M000211618

THE OLD CATHOLIC CHURCH
CHURCH
†
A HISTORY AND CHRONOLOGY

THIRD EDITION
REVISED AND EXPANDED

by

Bishop Karl Prüter

A St. Willibrord's Press Book

THE BORGO PRESS
An Imprint of Wildside Press

MMVI

The Autocephalous Orthodox Churches
ISSN 1059-1001
Number Three

Copyright © 1973, 1985, 1996, 2006 by Bishop
Karl Prüter
All rights reserved. No part of this book may be
reproduced in any form without the expressed
written consent of the publisher.

Published in the United States of America by
The Borgo Press, an imprint of Wildside Press,
P.O. Box 301, Holicong, PA 18928-0301

Library of Congress Cataloging for the Second Edition:

Prüter, Karl, 1920-
  The Old Catholic Church : a history and chronology / by Bishop Karl
Prüter. — 2nd ed., rev. and expanded.
   p. cm. — (The Autocephalous Orthodox churches, ISSN 1059-1001 ;
no. 3)
  Rev. and enl. ed. of: A history of the Old Catholic Church. 1985.
  Includes bibliographical references and index.
  1. Old Catholic Church—History. 2. Independent Catholic churches—
History. I. Prüter, Karl, 1920- . History of the Old Catholic Church. II.
Title. II. Series.
BX4765.P78 1996   95-3866
284'.8—dc20 CIP

THIRD EDITION

CONTENTS
†

List of Illustrations 4
Preface to the Third Edition 5
Old Catholic Church Chronology 9

1. The Early Church..13
2. The Reformation 19
3. The Old Catholic Church in Europe 25
4. The Oxford Movement......................................31
5. The Autocephalous Orthodox Churches..........37
6. The Old Catholic Church of England 43
7. The Roman Catholic Church in America........51
8. Joseph René Vilatte..59
9. Carmel Henry Carfora.....................................67
10. The Polish National Catholic Church 73
11. The African Orthodox Church........................81
12. The Free Catholic Movement 87
13. Christ Catholic Church 93
14. Christ Catholic Church International..............101
15. Other Old Catholic Bodies in America..........107

Notes...111
Bibliography..113
Index...117
About the Author..135

LIST OF ILLUSTRATIONS
(Courtesy of J. Gordon Melton)
✝

Archbishop Joseph Zielonka .... Cover
Bishop Karl Prüter 8
From left: Archbishop Vilatte, Mar Ivanios, Mar
    Dionysios, Mar Athanasios, Mar Gregorios,
    Mar Julius Alvarez 30
Archbishop Joseph René Vilatte 42
Archbishop Bernard Mary Williams (U.K.) 58
Bishops and Archbishops of the Polish National
    Catholic Church 92

PREFACE TO THE THIRD EDITION
†

Twenty years ago, I wrote and published *A History of the Old Catholic Church.* When I was asked by Borgo Press to revise the work which was now out-of-print, I readily agreed assuming it would be a relatively easy task. I realized the movement had grown, but I was aware neither of the extent of its growth nor the fact that it had found an entirely new constituency.

The revolution of the 1960s brought with it a spiritual resurgence that favored the Autocephalous Movement of the Churches of the Apostolic Succession. The new converts sought a spiritual experience within a structured framework, but one which was not associated with the "establishment." Further, the ethnic base of Old Catholicism continues to erode. The Polish National Catholic Church is in a state of decline. The principle cause is the shrinking of its ethnic base and its stubborn refusal to enter the American main stream. It also held itself aloof from other Old Catholics, refusing to recognize their legitimacy and not seeking their fellowship and cooperation. The African Orthodox Church has also declined, although it has always been willing to join in fellowship with other Old Catholics. Currently, there is a split between a group headed by Archbishop Stafford Sweeting, and one headed by Archbishop G. Duncan Hinkson. At this writing there are discussions between the two groups which may lead to reunion.

Two of the Churches which were small and struggling in 1973 have grown considerably. Both Christ Catholic Church and The Old Catholic Church of America have never catered to any particular ethnic group. Their growth has been slow but steady. A more recent jurisdiction which is growing steadily is the American Catholic Church under the leadership of Bishop Robert Allmen. It too is reaching out to a broad spectrum of people.

European Old Catholicism seems to be taking a strange turn. It has not grown but has become infected with the erosion of faith which many of the main line Protestant groups have experienced. The idea of women priests has been agreed upon, in principle, by a number of the National Old Catholic Churches on the Continent. It is still too early to evaluate the situation in Europe, but since no American Church has any link with those Churches, what happens in Europe should not greatly affect the situation here.

Finally, information about and communication between the various jurisdictions has greatly increased since 1973, with the publication of *The Old Catholic Sourcebook, Independent Bishops: An International Directory, The Directory of Bishops of the Autocephalous Churches of the Apostolic Succession*, and *The St. Willibrord Journal*. Although the various jurisdictions have shown little inclination to work together, they are, at least, aware of one another's existence. The author has found that among the jurisdictions which have viable parishes, there is a growing fraternal feeling. Those without valid apostolates continue to criticize the good works of others.

There is also a growing unity of faith and purpose as the indirect result of the new publications. Most Old Catholics have read *The Old Catholic Sourcebook*, *A History of the Old Catholic Church*, and *Bishops Extraordinary*. In addition many of them are using various publications of The St. Willibrord Press, such as: *The Confirmation Workbook and Catechism*, *The Catholic Priest*, *The Priest's Handbook*, *The Simple Service Book*, *The Divine Liturgy: The Mass for Orthodox Use*, and dozens of tracts and pamphlets. The use of this material stresses and strengthens the common faith which they hold.

It is my prayer that the next two decades will bring new growth and new unity and necessitate a Fourth Edition of this history.

+ Karl Prüter
Springfield, Missouri

THE OLD CATHOLIC CHURCH, BY KARL PRÜTER

OLD CATHOLIC CHURCH CHRONOLOGY
✝

4 BC   The birth of Jesus.

29?   The death and resurrection of Jesus.

1545   (through 1563) The Council of Trent. Separation of the Protestants from the Catholic Church.

1724   Consecration of Cornelius Steenoven as Archbishop of Utrecht by Bishop Dominique Marie Varlet.

1833   The Oxford Movement began.

1840   (through 1884) The Trustee Controversy in the American Catholic Church.

1866   Jules Ferrette, Bishop of Iona, publishes *The Eastern Liturgy Adapted for Use in the West*, and attempts to call Anglicans to Orthodoxy.

1869   (through 1870) Vatican Council I is held.

1871 Old Catholic Council is held at Munich: twenty-three "Old Catholic" parishes are formed.

1873 Josef Hubert Reinkens consecrated bishop for the German Old Catholic Church by Bishop Hermann Heykamp, Bishop of Deventer.

1892 The consecration of Joseph René Vilatte by Mar Julius I, bishop of the Independent Catholic Church of Ceylon, Goa, and India, to be the Old Catholic Bishop of America.

1897 Organization of the Polish National Catholic Church under the leadership of Father Francis Hodur.

1908 Consecration of Arnold Harris Mathew as Bishop of the Old Catholic Church of England by Bishop Gerardus Gul.

1910 Separation of the Old Catholic Church of England from Utrecht.

1916 Consecration of Carmel Henry Carfora as Bishop of the North American Old Roman Catholic Church by Bishop de Landas Berghes et de Rache.

1921 Consecration of Dr. George Alexander McGuire by Bishops Joseph René Vilatte and Carl A. Nybledh, as first bishop of the African Orthodox Church.

1937 Joseph Zielonka consecrated by Bishops as first bishop of the Polish Old Catholic Church, the name of which is changed in 1950 to Christ Catholic Church of the Americas and Europe.

1941 Founding of the Old Catholic Church of America by Bishop Francis X. Resch.

1967 Archbishop Peter Zhurawetzky approves Constitution and by-laws for Christ Catholic Church, Diocese of Boston. This autocephalous Church eventually assumed the name of Christ Catholic Church after Archbishop Zhurawetzky's group became defunct.

1989 Formation of the American Catholic Church—Old Catholic by Bishop Paul Raible.

1993 Union of Christ Catholic Church and the Liberal Catholic Church of Ontario. Archbishop (William) Donald Mullan is elected Presiding Bishop of Christ Catholic Church, International, the name of the united church.

1995 Christ Catholic Church and the Liberal Catholic Church of Ontario decide to go their separate ways. The two factions of the African Orthodox Church merge.

THE OLD CATHOLIC CHURCH, BY KARL PRÜTER

I.

THE EARLY CHURCH
†

In a remote corner of The Roman Empire during the reign of Tiberius Caesar, an event occurred that changed the whole world. The birth of Jesus, the son of a carpenter, came at a fortuitous time. For six hundred years prophets and philosophers had been attempting to teach men how to live. They set forth views on how the world came into being, the purpose and meaning of existence, and they attempted to give men standards by which to live. Many ideals were set forth, but things remained in a state of flux and men were uncertain and confused. The established religion of Judea had become static, and even the reform movement let by the Pharisaic sect had lost much of its vitality.

When Jesus reached manhood there were a few small signs of religious stirring. A small sect called the Essenes seemed to offer the challenge of the mystical life. Another group under John the Baptist, a cousin of Jesus, proclaimed the coming of a Jewish Messiah (savior). John's followers, although considerable, would hardly seem to herald any important upheaval in the Roman world. Of greater significance would be the fact that Judaism was gradually making inroads into the traditional gentile world. Wherever Jews emigrated, they established synagogues for their own people. The synagogue was a place of religious training and a place of worship. Soon many non-Jews were attracted to these places of learning and a growing number were converted to the faith.

A person seeking answers to life's basic questions and who sincerely searched for a way to live was not without choices in the Roman world. The philosophers, largely Greek, offered their complex systems of metaphysics and ethics. Many mystery cults flourished through the Middle East and even in the Eternal City itself. These ranged from the Zoroastrians, fire worshippers, to the followers of Mithra. The vast majority of people held some kind of nominal belief in the gods of Greece and Rome, and in the official worship of Caesar and the old Roman gods.

Judaism had a sophistication not found outside of these philosophical systems, and offered the added element of a monotheistic God who was concerned for mankind. What was missing was the actual presence of God among men. The Jewish world predicted and expected that God would make Himself manifest among men, but nevertheless, the Jews were unprepared for the event when it occurred.

Events in the tiny village of Bethlehem would soon turn the world upside down. People had come to the village in the reign of Caesar Augustus to be taxed. Among them was the family of Joseph and Mary, and while abiding there a child was born to

14

them who would be called Jesus. In time many
would hail Him as the long awaited Jewish Messiah.
Little is known of his childhood, but he apparently
followed his father's trade and labored as a carpenter. In his thirtieth year he went like many others to
hear his cousin, John the Baptist, preach. We are
told that Jesus then went into the wilderness to
meditate concerning his experience. Upon his emergence he began a ministry of teaching and healing.
Thousands came to hear him and many went away
convinced that they had seen and heard God in the
flesh. It soon became apparent that Christ intended
to stay among men and that a new era was opened in
history. Jesus wrote no books, made no new laws,
and unlike most religious teachers, set forth no new
principles for living. He brought men and women
into a living relationship with him. This living fellowship he referred to as His Body or the Church.
His subsequent crucifixion, death, and resurrection
were the final proof, if any was needed, that God
intended to remain in the world. Easter, the Day of
His Resurrection, became a great festival, and its
celebration separates those who accept the fact of
His Resurrection from those who do not.

For Old Catholics the meaning of Easter is clear
and it is simple. The Church is no less nor no more
than a group of people in a particular place who live
with Christ and who accept Him as their leader and
guide. Stripped of all that is nonessential, this is the
Church reduced to its Divine Essence. I doubt if
others would quarrel with this definition, although
in actual practice there are still too few of all faiths,
Old Catholics included, for whom this is a practical
and living reality.

Yet down through the ages saints, mystics, and small groups of devout people have satisfied themselves that they come into the presence of God whenever the Holy Sacrament is celebrated. For Christ had commanded his followers to "Do this for the recalling of me." Unfortunately, the more common translation, "This do in remembrance of me," has led many to observe the Supper as a mere memorial feast.

The Church also took on an institutional form, and many have mistaken the form for the substance. During the first century the Church consisted largely of small groups of believers who met in homes to seek Christ's presence in the celebration of the Holy Supper. They sought in fellowship with Him to live as the Holy Spirit directed them. Many entered the Church with little understanding, and with the Church's growth and increase in popularity, it became more and more difficult to maintain the simplicity of the Gospel of Jesus. Gradually, buildings had to be built to house the worshippers and a vast ecclesiastical structure was created to administer Church affairs. Unfortunately, it was patterned after the Roman Government, and many of the bishops began to imitate their counterparts in the Roman Government. But neither the buildings nor the ecclesiastical superstructure made any great difference to the devout, and it was not these people who were involved in the great controversies which swirled in and around the "institutional church." By the end of the fourth century the institutional church had evolved into a vast hierarchical structure which counted as its adherents almost the entire population of the Roman Empire. Five great centers of power

16

had developed, and the Bishops of Rome, Antioch, Alexandria, Jerusalem, and Constantinople vied for power and control.

Orthodoxy was determined by means of the Church Council. The Council of Nicaea was called together by Emperor Constantine to settle the Arian controversy. The Council brought together the leaders of the Church from every corner of the world. In seven councils over several centuries, the Church attempted to define what was orthodox and what was not. Those who failed to accept these decisions were branded as heretics and cast out of the Church. Critics of the Church have noted that the pious and the saintly were unable to influence the Councils or stem the tide of worldliness and materialism that marked so much of the Church. But it is equally noteworthy that none of this materialism and worldliness had any great influence upon those who accepted Jesus's words literally. Each age and each generation produced men and women who were aware that God was present in the world and who sought to order their lives and even their environment, when possible, according to His laws, and His direction. Occasionally it brought them into conflict with the institutional church, but surprisingly seldom. St. Augustine, Bishop of Hippo, was that rare exception of a saint in a place of influence, and he was able to shape the theological direction of the Western Church for many centuries.

THE OLD CATHOLIC CHURCH, BY KARL PRÜTER

II.

THE REFORMATION
†

During the Middle Ages the Church found her-self increasingly burdened with secular responsibili-ties. The Pope was not only the spiritual head of the Western Church, but by the Middle Ages he had be-come a secular ruler who also governed the Papal States, a small nation of which the City of Rome was the capital. As such he exacted taxes, his courts sent felons to jail, and he even, on many occasions, made war. His was just another feudal state, and in many respects he was just another feudal ruler.

During this time, the monasteries continued to grow and attracted thousands who chose to live in a cloistered world. Unfortunately, the cloisters were supported by having monks work the land. In the Middle Ages land was the principal form of wealth, and the Church's acquisition of so much acreage led to serious problems. The Church had become wealthy, and its wealth attracted to various church offices a host of people, whose main interest was in acquiring a share of her wealth and power.

By 1400 A.D. it was evident that a large part of the church was in the hands of ungodly men. The Council of Constance in 1414 attempted to deal with reform, but was sidetracked by the opposition that built up against John Hus and his attempts at reform. The reformers at Constance wanted many changes, but primarily they wanted dedicated leadership. They wanted the removal of immoral and avaricious priests and prelates. They hoped to limit the power of the papacy. Some wanted to abolish the granting of Indulgences (*i.e.*, the removal of certain church-imposed penalties for sin, in exchange for acts of grace including the gift of alms, endowments, and the like).

Ultimately, two groups of Reformers were successful. The Protestant Reformation under the leadership of Martin Luther created a permanent schism by splintering the Western Church into various separated denominations. The large bulk of Catholics, however, waited until the Council of Trent which met from 1545 to 1563. The Council of Trent was not simply a reaction to the Protestant Revolt; it was a genuine attempt at reform. As such, it was as successful as the Protestant counterpart. Many who had left the church earlier felt that they had been hasty, and in Bavaria and Austria, thousands returned to the fold.

Unfortunately, neither reformation dealt with the central concerns of Old Catholicism. Religious liberty was not practiced by either party, and its emergence seemed as unlikely in one group as in the other. Both sides of the Reformation looked to a council of the church rather than to the Papacy for authority. After Trent, however, the Roman Church tended to look more and more to the Papacy for direction, while the Protestants became more and more the people of the Book. The concept that Christ was among men and that the Church should be led by Him was yet to reappear. Men might plead that the individual must be guided by his conscience, but the thought that the entire church could be guided and directed by the living Christ did not re-emerge at this time.

Perhaps only a small group of dissenters could think of turning in this direction. About two hundred years after the Reformation, a small group of Jansenists fled France where the Jesuits were persecuting them and sought refuge in Holland. What the Jansenists believed and taught is not important in this discussion, but for the reader's information, they were a small group of Catholics who were anxious to restore to the church some of the asceticism of the past. The Dutch Church to whom they turned for sanctuary would hardly seem like a place to give sympathy for an asceticism of a by-gone day, but they were sympathetic to the plight of their fellow Catholics. It was demanded by Roman authorities that the Jansenists be sent back to France to await whatever justice their tormentors had in mind for them. It was the ancient Archepiscopal See of Utrecht that spoke in the Jansenist's defense in particular, and in defense of religious liberty in general.

The Dutch Church now had to find a *raison d'être* for its position. In defying Papal authority they had to find another basis for truth. Since their numbers were few, they could hardly hope to fare well at a Council of the Church. Since they were not

21

Protestants, they were not inclined to claim the supremacy of Scriptures over the Church.

* * * * * * *

There were no thinkers in the Movement who set forth some ancient principle on which the church could stand, but principles were formulated by the action of the See of Utrecht.

First, they were determined that Catholics would not persecute Catholics.

Second, they felt that the Church in Holland must act as they felt Christ wished them to, even though both the Papacy and a Council were to condemn them. In effect, it was not their words but their actions which gave rise to Old Catholic doctrine.

They felt bound to their fellow Catholics through Christ.

They held the same faith.

They celebrated the same Sacraments.

They believed in the same Jesus Christ, as Lord and Savior. Their clergy held the same valid orders.

Therefore, it was Christ and not the Papacy nor the Councils that brought them together. Hence, in spite of Papal Excommunication, they would notify the Pope of each election and consecration of an Old Catholic Bishop.

No human act could sever the ties that bound Christ's people together. Therefore, re-unification is a misnomer since no separation was ever made. It was Rome that refused to recognize that all Catholics are brothers. The unity of the church as it pertains to Roman and Old Catholics requires no formal action on the part of Old Catholics. Rome on her part did take formal action in 1967, when she publicly rescinded her condemnation of the See of Utrecht. Since then this action has been implemented by some common cooperative projects. In Rotterdam an Old Catholic and a Roman Catholic parish united in a single parish that is effectively witnessing to Catholic unity.

III.

THE OLD CATHOLIC CHURCH IN EUROPE
†

During the latter part of the seventeenth century, a group of devout Catholics located at Port Royal in France who followed Cornelius Jansen, found themselves declared heretics of the Church. In seventeen-century France there was no place for Christians whose orthodoxy had been questioned by the Papacy. Hence, many of them fled for their lives to other lands where they would find more tolerance, or, at least, a government less efficient in the art of harassing heretics.

Thousands found their way into Holland, but the long arm of the Papacy sought to molest them even there. The army of the Papacy was the Jesuit Order, and they were anxious to harass the Port Royal, or Jansensist, heretics wherever they found them. In Holland, however, the See of Utrecht was most uncooperative. The Dutch insisted on sheltering the Jansenists, not out of sympathy for their ideas, but primarily out of human compassion and, perhaps, some antipathy towards the Jesuits.

25

Needless to say, a struggle for power began, since the Jesuits were determined to get their way in this matter. Archbishop van Neercassel of Utrecht soon found it necessary to travel to Rome to defend himself against the charge of heresy. In this he was completely successful and returned to Holland vindicated and a popular hero.[1]

Upon the death of Archbishop van Neercassel, Rome refused to approve the consecration of a new bishop for Utrecht. From this point forward the struggle between the Dutch churches and Rome was over the issue of authority. Rome contended it had the right to abolish the See of Utrecht and the Dutch churchmen held that it had no such right. Without an archbishop, the churches of the See had to obtain episcopal functions more or less sub-rosa. For a number of years, their candidates for the ministry were ordained by Bishop Fagan, Roman Catholic Bishop of Meath (Ireland).[2]

An unexpected solution to their problem was found in the person of Dominique Marie Varlet, who was consecrated in Paris as Bishop of Babylon. On the way to take up his duties, he stayed for a few days in Amsterdam. While there one of the parish priests, Jacob Krys, persuaded him to confirm 604 children who could not travel to other countries to be confirmed. Shortly after, he continued his journey and arrived in Persia on October 9, 1719. In March of the following year, he was suspended from office, and one of the reasons cited was the confirmation performed in Amsterdam. He then returned to Amsterdam, where he decided he would study and petition to have his suspension repealed. In the meantime, the Dutch continued to seek a

26

bishop for their vacant See, but without avail. Finally they elected Cornelius Steenoven to be archbishop, and prevailed upon the Bishop of Babylon to consecrate him on October 15, 1724.[3]

The new Archbishop duly announced his consecration to the Bishop of Rome, Pope Benedict XIII, who responded by declaring his consecration illicit. From this day on the Archbishopric of Utrecht was to be separate from Rome, and it, together with the Sees of Haarlam and Deventer, would be the first Old Catholic Churches.

In less than 150 years, a similar movement would get under way in Germany, Austria, and Switzerland. This time, however, the issue would not be so concerned with practical church administration, but with its theory. Pope Pius IX called the Vatican Council to meet in Rome in 1869. It was the most important council of the Roman Catholic Church since the Council of Trent, and it was called for the express purpose of proclaiming the Doctrine of Papal Infallibility.

Opposition to its proclamation began even before the council met and created a widespread controversy. When it was put to a vote after much bitter debate, some 451 bishops voted for it; sixty-two voted for it with reservations, and eighty-eight voted against it.[4] Most of the opponents were from German speaking lands, although at least one Italian and one American bishop, Fitzgerald of Little Rock, were numbered with them. Shortly, thereafter, the Council dispersed for the summer, but the Franco-Prussian War broke out and the Pope never summoned the Council to reconvene.

The bishops of the opposition had agreed before they left Rome to do nothing without consulting one another, but the war made this pledge impossible to keep. Eventually they were all to submit to Rome, although some did it with great *"restricto mentalis."*

However, many of the lower clergy and the laity were not so willing to submit to a dogma that they considered to be unorthodox. In the ensuing struggle, many who opposed the doctrine were excommunicated. Included were Ignaz von Döllinger, Chaplain to King Ludwig II of Bavaria and a foremost scholar. Döllinger and others continued to hold to what they called the "Old Catholic" position.

To them the situation was quite simple. The Vatican Council had introduced new and heretical ideas into the Church, and they would oppose them with whatever means they had at their disposal. In 1871, they called a council to be held in Munich, and it was the first of a long series of Old Catholic Councils.[5]

By the end of 1871, there were twenty-three Old Catholic congregations in Germany and Austria, and the movement was well on its way. By June they were ready to elect a bishop and chose Josef Hubert Reinkens, who was consecrated by Hermann Heykamp, the Bishop of Deventer. Thus the two movements, born in different places a century and a half apart, were brought together in Christian communion and in working relationship.

There were other Old Catholic communities that came into being at various times in Poland, Czechoslovakia, France, Yugoslavia, and other countries of Europe. However, it is the German and Dutch movements that directly affected the English and

American movements and hence, we have limited our study to these two.

IV.

THE OXFORD MOVEMENT
†

During the eighteenth century, English church life had been radically changed by the impact of the Methodist Movement. With its great emphasis upon a personal religious awakening, Methodism had succeeded in bringing to thousands a new commitment and a new zeal for Christian living. It created a vital new denomination and had affected the theology and life of almost every religious denomination in England.

Its effect on the Anglican church was to bring it a new vitality and to alter it beyond recognition. Initially, the Methodists brought back into an active relationship with the Church, many thousands of souls, particularly from among the lower classes. A schism became inevitable, for the church now had two competing theologies held by two distinct classes. The new members, recruited largely from the poor embraced the evangelical theology of the Methodist preachers, while those who had been members of the Church before the Methodist or Evangelical Movement were largely upper class and

31

had a more Catholic orientation. When the schism came, most people remained in the Church of England parishes. Only if a Methodist chapel was erected in the same parish would the question of choice come up. Even then, many would remain in the established Church either out of conviction, convenience, or fear of social approbation.

For the Church of England, this challenge proved a mixed blessing. The disruption of churches and parishes was not without harmful effect. The newcomers that remained were both a source of strength and an inherent weakness. Some had come into the Church as the result of a type of preaching and emotional appeal which was alien to the Established Church. Not finding it within their own parishes, they tended to judge the churches and the preachers critically. However, in spite of this there remained a vital evangelical or low-church party which sought to reshape the Church after the Methodist revival. When the people were in agreement, they succeeded in the creation of vital local parishes. They also created a faction which was to engage in a perpetual struggle with the high church party that was eventually to arise in the nineteenth century. To some, it appeared that this struggle was forever sapping the strength of the Church of England, but to others this same struggle appeared to keep the Church responsive and aware. It was this energy which strengthened her and allowed a response to contemporary needs.

In a sense, the Methodist Revival can be said to be the cause for the high church movement, or as it came to be known, "The Oxford Movement." At the beginning of the nineteenth century, men like Richard Hurrell Froude, John Henry Newman, and John Keble[6] looked at the Church of England and found her wanting. Methodism had altered it in many ways which disturbed them. First, there was in the Methodist Movement an anti-intellectualism that was to mark the Movement both in England and America. The Methodists did not seriously challenge the theology of the Church as such, but merely lessened the value of theologians and their speculations. What a man experienced was so vastly more important than what he believed that theological learning seemed to many to be an idle waste of time. In fact, many later proponents of the Evangelical Revival began to take a critical view of theological learning and to regard it as the work of the devil himself.

Secondly, although John Wesley, one of the early leaders of the Methodist Movement, was personally inclined towards liturgical worship, the very methods he used to win converts tended to make liturgy take a back seat. Since preaching was often done in the fields, in the mines, and in the factories, the situation did not lend itself to liturgical worship, and liturgy began to appear superfluous. At least, the thousands won to the Church through Evangelical preaching were not trained in worship and did not know what to make of it. The result was that the Methodists strengthened the puritan party within the Church and the last remnants of Catholic worship began to disappear.

These were not the only questions that the Anglo-Catholic reformers raised, but they were probably the two most significant factors that caused them to pose questions in the first place. To Richard Hurrell Froude such matters as fasting, clerical celi-

33

bacy, reverence for the saints, and "Catholic usages" were all matters of concern.

A third concern of Froude, Newman, and Keble was the Erastian nature of the English Church. Like the ideas of the Separatist Robert Browne before them, their concern was rooted in the belief that only by separating the Church from the State could the church return to primitive Christianity. The banner they raised was to attract thousands of adherents and to divide the Anglican Church into its present-day three factions: high, broad, and low church. The Anglo-Catholic Party, as it came to be called, emphasized two factors in church life that were to be of great influence in the emergence of Old Catholicism. First was the liturgical revival. The Anglo-Catholics wanted to return to the forms and ceremonies of Catholicism, partially to restore decency and order to worship and partially to return to the old traditions. Also, they suspected that the rejection of much of the ancient liturgy was also a rejection of the catholic doctrines which they expressed. The Anglo-Catholics also lay stress on the historic episcopate and the validity of Catholic orders.

As the Anglo-Catholic Movement grew, many of its adherents, particularly among the clergy, began to doubt the "catholicity" of the Church of England. On October 9, 1845, John Henry Newman made his submission to Rome, and was shortly followed by several hundred clergy and laymen. Most of these early defectors left because they looked at the Anglican Church and saw that their attempts to introduce catholic doctrine and practices had touched but a small portion of the Church. Where the whole Church was concerned, their teachings

34

were apt to be so watered down or compromised with Protestantism as to be barely recognizable. Since the Anglican church could not unite on a body of doctrine, it continued to contribute many of its Evangelicals to the various Protestant sects and its high churchmen to Rome. However, not all of the high churchmen, however dissatisfied with the Church of England, were prepared to submit to Rome. They remained within the Church but began to look elsewhere for evidence of a Catholic Church that had not been corrupted by "papal errors."

The Anglican Church had not yet fully recovered from the defection of John Henry Newman and his followers, when a second blow came. Pope Leo XIII declared in his bull *Apostolicae Curae* on September 13, 1886, that due to the rupture in apostolic succession, Anglican Orders were now invalid.[7] The Tractarian Movement, having stressed the necessity for each priest and bishop to be ordained or consecrated by a bishop in the "apostolic succession," was now in a quandary.

Leo's decision forced those concerned about apostolic succession either to acknowledge Rome or to find some means by which to obtain valid orders. For most of these high churchmen, the Oxford Movement had provided a satisfactory religious experience. They felt free to follow the ancient liturgy, offer the ancient prayers, believe and preach the catholic doctrines, and live according to catholic principles.

For many, however, the movement raised as many questions as it answered. Obviously, the Anglican Church lacked a unity of doctrine and practice that would be a necessary mark of a truly

35

Catholic Church. It was difficult for many to labor yoked together with Protestants and latitudinarians. The question of apostolic succession was to disturb many more clergymen than laymen, and it would continue to disrupt the Church for decades to come.

V.

THE AUTOCEPHALOUS ORTHODOX CHURCHES
†

In the 1840s a renewal of intercourse between Anglicans and Eastern Christians was undertaken by William Palmer, a deacon and a fellow of Magdalen College.[8] He journeyed to Russia to explore the possibility of inter-communion with the Orthodox Churches. Like many Anglicans who have ventured down this road ever since, he was disappointed when the Russians refused to admit him to the sacraments. Palmer's trip accomplished nothing, but it was a beginning of many similar trips and overtures to the Eastern Churches. In 1857, a handful of high churchmen established the Association for the Promotion of the Unity of Christendom. Six years later, with the blessing of Dr. Neale, the Eastern Church Association came into being.

In the midst of concern for Eastern recognition there appeared Jules Ferrette, a Frenchman bearing the title of Bishop of Iona who claimed to have been consecrated a bishop of the Syrian Jacobite Church. Like many of his successors, Ferrette was formerly a Roman Catholic priest. Shortly after he was raised to the priesthood, he joined the Dominican Mission in Mesopotamia and Kurdistan. Less than a year later, he renounced his Catholic faith and became a Presbyterian minister. Not much is known about his work in the Near East, and no documentary evidence has ever been uncovered to substantiate his claims to have been consecrated a bishop. What he claimed was that under the sanction of the then Syrian Patriarch of Antioch, Mar Ignatius Jacob II (Ighnatiyus Ya'qub in Arabic), the Bishop of Emesa (Homs) not only consecrated him a bishop, but dispatched him as Patriarchal Legate for Western Europe with the authority to erect indigenous Syrian Orthodox Churches. These churches were to function under an autonomous Patriarchate, not in any way subject to Antioch.[9]

The debate concerning the validity of these claims still goes on. At the same time there were many within the Anglican community that accepted them at face value. There were an equal number of Anglican high churchmen, including Dr. Pusey, who eyed them with a great degree of skepticism.

What Jules Ferrette, the Bishop of Iona, did was to offer to "lead" a movement toward the reunion of Christendom in England. More disturbing to the Established Church was the fact that he created, on English soil, another church claiming to be catholic, which called itself the Holy Catholic, Apostolic, Orthodox Church. In 1866, he published a book entitled, *The Euchologion of The Eastern Liturgy Adapted for Use in the West*, in which he offered "to give Holy Orders to pious and learned men who, being duly elected, will declare themselves willing to conform to this liturgy."[10] What the Bishop of Iona was proposing was soon made clear. He began the practice of ordaining English clergymen who doubted the validity of their own Anglican orders. Obviously, in many cases these men preferred to have the ordination performed *sub rosa* rather than reveal their inner doubts to their own superiors who might take a dim view of such ordinations.

The resultant controversy resulted in a permanent breach with the Church of England. By December 15, 1866, Ferrette denounced his critics in the English church and resolved to go his own way.[11] He had one loyal convert, and this was the Rev. Richard Williams Morgan. Morgan was a Welsh nationalist and a priest in the Church of England. He held many unusual ideas, including the notion that the Druidic Order was a forerunner of Christianity.

Ferrette's choice of Iona as the seat of his episcopate pleased Morgan and soon the two began to work hand in hand. In 1874 Morgan was conditionally baptized, confirmed, ordained and consecrated a bishop by Mar Julius, Bishop of Iona.[12] Shortly after this event, Ferrette faded out of the picture, and so to all practical purposes out of the church which he attempted to establish.

What did not disappear was Ferrette's idea. Others soon came along to follow in his footsteps. Nor long after his break with the Church of England another lapsed Roman Catholic priest, Dr. J. Joseph Overbeck, proposed the idea of an Orthodox Western Catholic Church. Overbeck sought the good offices of the Russian Patriarchate in this attempt; and while at times he seemed to come close to obtaining

39

recognition of his ideas, like Ferrette, he failed. Others, including Stephen Georgeson Hatherly, Ambrose Phillips de Lisle, and Ulric Vernon Herford, attempted to establish either Orthodox or Uniate Churches.

Herford did have some small measure of success. He managed to organize the Evangelical Catholic Church and a "Society of Free Catholics," the latter group being composed largely of Free Church ministers, many of whom sought orders from Ulric Vernon Herford. His most illustrious convert was Dr. William Orchard, pastor of Kings Weigh House. Kings Weigh House was a Congregational Church located in the heart of London, and Dr. Orchard while serving as pastor of the Church brought radical changes in its mode of worship, practices, and theology. During his ministry there the Church became Catholic and it only lacked a pastor with valid orders. Bishop Herford offered to ordain William Orchard its pastor, and thereby make him a Catholic priest with orders in the apostolic succession. In November of 1916 Bishop Herford conditionally baptized and confirmed William Orchard and then ordained him to the priesthood.[13]

The congregation at Kings Weigh House not only accepted the ordination, but was supportive of the step. Father Orchard continued for many years at Kings Weigh House, and during his ministry wrote many solid theological works and an outstanding book of prayer, which he entitled, *The Temple.* Eventually, he left the Congregational Church and was received as a layman in the Roman Catholic Church, where he continued to write theological books and his monumental autobiography, *From Faith to Faith*.

Bishop Herford's other legacy was the Evangelical Catholic Church, which functions even today in both England and America. It is a small group, with more priests than laity. It meets the Anglo-Catholic desire for liturgy and for valid orders.

In faith it seems to be a mixture of Orthodoxy, Catholicism, and Protestantism. Since this group, like many of its kind, has no recognized body of dogma or doctrine, it is held together largely by its ritual and the personalities of its leaders.

In recent years followers of this group have tended to identify themselves as often with Old Catholicism as with Orthodoxy. However, we shall see in the next two chapters that their origins are quite different. What they do have in common is their appeal to the same groups of people who seem to share the same religious needs.

The Old Catholic Church, by Karl Prüter

VI.

THE OLD CATHOLIC CHURCH OF ENGLAND
†

The First Vatican Council, had, as we have seen shaken the European Church to its roots. While the numbers who gathered at the Congress of Munich were small, the challenge which they issued was to challenge the Catholic Church for decades to come. The twenty-three parishes which chose to become Old Catholic made other Catholics the world over realize that one did not have to be a part of the Papal Church to be truly Catholic.

Watching the events in Munich were many of the high churchmen in the Church of England, and telegrams and letters were received at the Congress of Munich from the Bishop of Ely and the Bishop of Lincoln; the Rev. F. S. May attended the congress with commendatory letters from both bishops. Anglo-Catholics as a whole rejoiced, since it underscored the vital truth that one could be truly Catholic without submitting to the Pope.

Most important of the distant observers was Arnold Harris Mathew. At the time the Old Catholics were getting underway in the German countries, he was studying for the Anglican ministry. However, doubts soon assailed him, and he soon left and entered the Roman Catholic Seminary of St. Peter's at Partickhill, Glasgow. Eighteen months later he was ordained a priest and began to serve various parishes in the Roman Church. This lasted until July, 1889, when he informed his parishioners that he doubted Papal Infallibility. Next he served Unitarian parishes, and this lasted about twelve months. He once again offered his services to the Church of England, and was permitted to serve as curate at Holy Trinity on Sloane Street, London. While he was there, he married one Margaret Duncan, an act well received by his Anglican parishioners.

When the rector left Holy Trinity "under a cloud" in 1890, Mathew decided to turn his back on the Church of England once more and return to lay status. He went into secular work and tried to regain his status in the Roman Church. In this he was completely unsuccessful, and so he tried to support his family as best he could. He turned to literary work and he managed to edit, translate, and write a few books. However, he was never happy as a layman, and continually sought ways and means to regain his status as a priest. He approached various Anglican Bishops without success, and finally in 1907, he began to correspond with Edward Herzog, the Christian Catholic Bishop of Switzerland.

What Arnold Harris Mathew told Bishop Herzog and later the Old Catholic Bishops of Holland was essentially true. He stated that many Anglo-Catholics who feared the Report of the Ritual Commission set up in 1904 would welcome an Old

Catholic Church of England. He also correctly stated that a number of Roman Catholic priests wished to embrace the tenets of the Old Catholic Communities of Germany and Switzerland. He did, however, conceal from the Dutch Old Catholics his marital status, and by implication, he vastly exaggerated the size of his following in England. When his marriage was made known to the Dutch, they were horrified, but in spite of this and in spite of Anglican objections, they consecrated Arnold Harris Mathew on April 28, 1908.[14]

Having received episcopal consecration, Bishop Mathew returned to England to build his Church. While he may have exaggerated his following, it must be said in his defense that he was more of a victim than a villain. One Father Richard O'Halloran had been responsible for the claim that seventeen priests with eight fully-organized parishes were ready to follow Arnold Mathew. When the Bishop discovered he had been duped, he wrote to Archbishop Gul of Utrecht and stated the facts accurately. The facts were that Bishop Mathew would have to build a church almost from the ground up. There were, to be sure, priests both in the Anglican and the Roman Churches who were ready to follow him, but in almost no instance could they bring their congregations with them.

One of the first converts was the Rev. W. Noel Lambert, pastor of the Congregational Chapel in River Street, Islington. He was ordained a deacon and priest, and he soon placed his chapel at Bishop Mathew's disposal. It was dedicated to St. Willibrord and consecrated as a pro-cathedral.[15] On June 13, 1910, Mathew took the step that brought about a

45

breech with Utrecht. He consecrated two excommunicated Roman Catholic priests as bishops without notifying the other Old Catholic bishops.

The resultant storm finally caused Mathew to write a "Declaration of Autonomy and Independence" which was printed in *The Guardian* on January 6, 1911.

Now the Old Catholic Church of England was an independent body, free to perform any ecclesiastical function without consulting Utrecht. It was small, as parishes existed only in Chiswick, Croyden, Broadstairs, Belfast, Oxford, and Islington. Growth of the new church was painfully slow, and by and large, high-church Anglicans kept clear of it. Bishop Mathew was not entirely happy with his self-imposed exile, and sought about for some Catholic or Orthodox group with whom he could be in communion. The answer came on August 5, 1911, when the Orthodox Patriarch of Antioch, Gregory IV, agreed to receive the English Catholic Church (Mathew's new name for his church) into Union. The practical effect of this upon the growth of the Old Catholic Church in England was nil, but it probably gave some of its followers the satisfaction of knowing that one of the ancient patriarchs recognized them as an Orthodox Christian body.

This recognition, however, came none too soon; for in the summer of 1914, Bishop Mathew received into the English Catholic Church the Rev. Frederick Samuel Willoughby, an Anglican clergyman of dubious character. Willoughby had a great deal of ability, and Bishop Mathew found him congenial to work with and extremely able. Within a short time he raised Willoughby to the episcopate. It was not long before he learned how seriously he had blundered. Bishop Willoughby was a convinced theosophist, and had already won many of the clergy in the English Catholic Church to his views. Many of the members of the English Catholic Church (by now it was renamed the Old Roman Catholic Church) were now members of the Theosophical Society. Indeed, Bishop Mathew had given permission to continue his active work in the Theosophical Society to one of his priests, Father Wedgwood.

By the time Mathew got around to condemning the theosophical heresy, Bishop Willoughby and his group were in control of the Church. On the feast of the Transfiguration, August 6, 1915, Bishop Mathew condemned the theosophists in a pastoral letter. The result was that most of the churches went with the Willoughby group to form the Liberal Catholic Church.

Small as the Old Catholic Church, English Catholic Church, and Old Roman Catholic Church had been, it was now reduced to a state of shambles. Its recovery has been slow and considerably hampered by various schisms. By the mid-1960s England had not one but at least a dozen churches in the Mathew succession. Many of them had also established branches in the United States and even in Europe. Today there are jurisdictions with such names as Catholic Apostolic Church, Celtic Catholic Church of the Utrecht Succession, Old Roman Catholic Church, Ancient Catholic Church, Free Catholic Church, and Old Catholic Church of England. There are many bishops, priests, and deacons in these denominations, but very few laymen. Most parishes that have no more than a half dozen people, mostly clergy, to worship at Sunday morning Mass.

This is not what Bishop Mathew visualized or promised when he went to Utrecht. It did not fulfill the hopes and expectations of vast hordes of dissident Anglicans. But it continues, as do the other autocephalous Orthodox and now Anglican jurisdictions as well, to be a refuge for the occasional Anglican priest who doubts his church's catholicity or orders. These small groups often gather in a few dissident Catholics unhappy over Vatican II, or Anglicans disturbed by the ordination of women or the abandonment of the traditional Anglican liturgy.

From the foregoing, I have come to several conclusions regarding Old Catholicism in England. First, this movement is not in any real sense an importation from the Continent, but rather an indigenous church. The same drives and motives which caused many men to create autocephalous Orthodox Churches caused Bishop Mathew and others to create an Old Catholic Church on English soil. I draw this conclusion, in part, from my study of the Oxford Movement and those who broke with it, in part from my study of the autocephalous Orthodox Churches, and finally, from my study of the history of the Old Catholic Church of England. Bishop Mathew sought Orthodox recognition with simple ease after his break with Utrecht. In short, to Mathew, one was as good as the other and served the self-same ends.

Finally, the *raison d'être* of Old Catholicism in England is to be found in its liturgy and in its "valid" orders. It is not in doctrine, since no two of the present Old Catholic bodies agree in doctrine or

48

could even tell you what their doctrinal position is. The closest they come is to state negatively that it is not theosophy, having driven the theosophists out, and they add that it is Catholic because they accept the ancient creeds and the ancient councils of the Universal Church.

THE OLD CATHOLIC CHURCH, BY KARL PRÜTER

VII.

THE ROMAN CATHOLIC CHURCH IN AMERICA
✝

The first Catholics in America were members of the Roman Church. The earliest missions on this continent were planted by Spanish and later by French missionaries. Even in the English settlements the Spanish and French clergy predominated for over a century. It was only gradually that a French hierarchy was displaced by an Irish hierarchy. The work that they did lacked nothing in zeal, and for the most part they did their work well. But because Americans came from many different national backgrounds, the tendency first of the French and later of the Irish to monopolize Holy Orders created serious problems.

The Church was further handicapped by the fact that she found herself in a hostile Protestant environment. Even when she did not encounter hostility, the culture was so Protestant in character that often the Church tended to adopt ways which were alien to her own character. Because the laws in most states placed the ownership of Church property in

51

the hands of lay trustees, the Catholic were for the most part forced to go along with that system of ownership for its church buildings.

Catholics were regarded as somewhat alien, and the popular feeling was the Catholicism was not in harmony with the democratic spirit of the new nation. Hence, few Catholic prelates were inclined to protest the system of lay trustees which seemed to be democratic in principle and the accepted way of doing things in American society. Nor is there anything in the system that is inconsistent with Catholic ideals or faith. The Episcopate, including Archbishop John Carroll, accepted it and fully expected that it would work.[16] It was difficult in the eighteenth century to visualize how the various ethnic quarrels would use and misuse the system. Even in Carroll's day, the threat to set up an "Independent Catholic Church of America" was heard. All kinds of things motivated such talk, and it was not so much anti-Papal as anti-French and anti-Irish.

Theodore Maynard contends that the system could not work for the Catholic Church because Catholic Churches were less "exclusive" than Protestant Churches. He contends that the trustees in Protestant Churches were almost always men of good standing in the community, while Catholic Churches in the eighteenth and nineteenth centuries had few substantial citizens from which to draw. While Protestant Churches limited the franchise to "confirmed" members in good standing, Catholic Churches (under canon law) gave full privileges to all baptized members. Often it was the most lax lay members who sought to be elected as trustees, and since they had little knowledge of Catholic life they were easily led by insubordinate clergymen and laymen. Further, while democracy was clearly the wave of the future in the land, Rome was slow in granting independence to her American children. The American clergy were anxious to elect their own bishops, but Rome for decades seemed reluctant to permit this. Consequently, not a few Catholics felt torn by what seemed like undemocratic procedures in their church while, as patriots, they felt inclined to espouse the cause of democracy in secular and in church life. Trusteeism lasted longer than it needed to because it became a symbol for the democracy which so many Catholics felt was lacking in the church.

It must be remembered that the American Catholic was in an unusual situation. He had come from an old part of the world where everything was settled and established. The church in which he had worshipped had stood there for centuries. Not only did he not build it, but it was bought and paid for long before he came into the world. In America he had a struggle to establish himself personally. Often he came without family and after years of work and saving was able to send enough money back to bring the wife and children across the ocean. In addition, he was asked to help build a church. Frequently, he gave generously, not only of money, of which he had little, but often of his time and labor. Many a simple frame Catholic Church stood out on the prairie as the result of labor that was donated and materials bought with the pennies of the immigrant congregation.

It is not surprising that they wanted to own it, and felt that the stewardship of God's property should be entrusted to those whose labor had provided it. The law of the land also decreed that they should own the church, and when disputes came between the bishops and the people, the courts threw their weight on the side of the people. Further, the quarrel was complicated by the nature of the lower clergy. Many of the priests were the rejects of Europe. If any Irish or French bishop wanted to get rid of a priest he often suggested, not too subtly, that the place for him was the mission fields of America.

These men found a new security in the American trustee system. If they could seal themselves to their congregations, they could live as they choose without interference from the bishop. By the same token, it became the congregation that called the tune. If they were displeased with the priest, they could, and they often did, withhold his salary. Finally, the multi-racial system almost made trusteeism a necessity. A German congregation was not easily persuaded to turn over the fruits of their labor to an Irish or a French bishop. If they had a priest of their own nationality, he preferred their authority to that of the bishop.

A typical example is the case of Caesarius Reuter, a German, who was stationed at St. Peter's in Baltimore. Father Reuter did not relish being an assistant, and so asked Bishop Carroll for permission to work among the German immigrants.[17] Everything was fine until Father Reuter decided he wanted to organize a separate parish for Germans. When Bishop Carroll did not agree, Father Reuter claimed racial prejudice and went to Rome to ask that a German bishop be appointed for America.

54

When his plea was dismissed, Father Reuter returned to Baltimore and gathered a schismatic congregation. Bishop Carroll was quite capable of meeting the challenge and he was not long in asserting his authority over all the Catholics in his diocese.

A more dramatic and perhaps the most serious quarrel at this time centered around Archbishop Ambrose Marechal. As Archbishop of Baltimore, he viewed his Irish parishioners with some distaste. They, in turn, mistrusted his French ways and resented his authority. This was a situation which a few opportunistic priests used to create considerable disorder. One of these was Dr. Simon Felix Gallagher, who had a reputation both as a preacher and as a drinker. Father Gallagher was liked by his congregation, but he had several times been admonished by his bishop. That he was a likable fellow there is no doubt since he was supported by a fellow Irishman of note, Canon Robert Browne, an Augustinian who was determined to defend Father Gallagher all the way. Finally, both Gallagher and Browne were suspended by Archbishop Neale; although suspended, Gallagher managed to retain control of St. Mary's and promptly appealed his case to Rome.[18]

It is difficult to know how much support Gallagher and Browne had, but it must have been considerable. Browne went to Rome to plead their case and at first, Propaganda upheld them. The death of Neale complicated the case and brought the two Irishmen face to face with the Frenchman, Marechal. What happened is difficult to clearly determine. In his history of *American Catholicism*,

55

Theodore Maynard tells of a letter sent on January 4, 1819, to a Franciscan named Haves in Dublin. It presumably came from a group in Charleston, S.C., who were dissatisfied with the state of affairs in the Church. They wanted Haves to go to Utrecht and have himself consecrated Bishop of South Carolina. He was offered money and support. All they asked in return was that he would come to America and there consecrate other bishops.

All of this sounds very bizarre. We have no way of knowing why they would send the letter to Haves, who reported their plot to his superiors, and what basis they had for believing that Utrecht would grant their request. Further, they sent no money for Haves's expenses. Perhaps the whole plot was hatched for the purpose of creating a scare. If such was their intent they were successful, and Rome proceeded to act. Propaganda decided that they could not hope to maintain the church in the South without Irish bishops. They found two whom they thought would be able to restore order to the chaotic American Church. Patrick Kelly was chosen for Richmond and John England for Charleston. The appointment of England marked a new beginning for the Church in America, and for a time postponed the emergence of an Independent Catholic Church. Bishop England had a feeling and a love for democracy, and proceeded to Americanize the Catholic Church in the United States. He proceeded to deal with the problem of trusteeism by seeming to accept it. In 1833 he proposed a new constitution for his diocese, incorporating the idea of trusteeship, but pulling a few of its sharper teeth by creating a presbyterian system of diocesan government. Whether it was England's reforms or his personality that won the day is debatable, but he succeeded in bringing order not only to his diocese, but also to much of the American Church.

Although much of the Catholic Church was not ready to accept Bishop England's solution, his voice raised the hopes of those who wanted a more democratic church sufficiently to prevent any serious schismatic movements. In the next decade the disturbances in the church were either of the orderly type that took place in the councils of the church between the faction led by Bishop Marechal and Bishop England, or squabbles between a few difficult priests and their bishops. There were none of major importance. The church was to enjoy a period of relative peace until the great tide of immigration following the Civil War.

VIII.

JOSEPH RENÉ VILATTE
✝

Throughout America there were many Catholics who were discontented, neglected, or simply adopting new ideas in their new-found environment. Until the turn of the Century, most of the discontented found expression in strife by quarreling with their clergy, although often it spread to conflict between individual parishes and their bishops. Occasionally, an individual priest or parish separated from the Roman jurisdiction, but these were isolated incidents and did not constitute a movement away from Rome.

Joseph René Vilatte was not the cause of the discontent, and was never a leader of any appreciable number of dissatisfied Catholics, but he did bring before American Catholics the challenge of Old Catholicism. As we said earlier, from time to time discontented parishes had thought of turning to Utrecht, but little or nothing was done. It remained for Vilatte to lead the way. He was born in Paris, France on January 24, 1854, of parents who belonged to the Petite Église, an independent Catholic

59

body dating from Napoleonic times.[19] However, the group was dying out, and Joseph Vilatte was reared in the Roman Catholic Church. In due course he entered the Community of Christian Brothers in Namur, Belgium, but after a short stay emigrated to Canada. Here he entered the College of Saint-Laurent in Montréal, and began his studies for the priesthood. While at Montréal, he heard about the lapsed priest, Father Charles Chiniquy, and after three years of study at Saint-Laurent he decide to leave. For a time he retired to the Clerics of St. Viator at Bourbonnais, Illinois.

Once again he came in contact with Father Chiniquy, and, at his suggestion, went to Wisconsin to work among the Belgians. He also began to write to Hyacinthe Loyson, a lapsed Discalced Carmelite Friar who had formed a church in France called the Gallican Catholic Church. For some reason, he began his work in Wisconsin as a free-lance "Presbyterian" missionary. He was not particularly successful, and quickly saw that the Belgians, although they had strayed from Rome, were not about to become Presbyterians. It was probably on the advice of Hyacinthe Loyson that he approached the Episcopal church so that he could continue his work among the Belgians as an "Old Catholic." He proposed that the Anglicans help him secure Old Catholic Orders in Europe, and then, upon his return, he would engage in missionary work under the direction of the Anglican Church.

However, the arrangement was never clearly defined and in time difficulties developed. He was ordained deacon and priest by Bishop Herzog of Switzerland on June 6 and 7, 1885.[20] Upon his return to

Wisconsin, he opened the mission Church of the Precious Blood in Little Sturgeon and later a second mission in Green Bay, the Church of the Blessed Sacrament. Blessed Sacrament Church eventually became an Episcopal Church and is still active in that denomination. For three years Vilatte labored successfully in Wisconsin. He had with him one Father Gauthier, a Swiss Old Catholic, and between them they served three churches at Little Sturgeon, Green Bay, and Dyckesville.

Unfortunately, Father Vilatte was a restless soul and was not content to serve as a simple parish priest. He had received a letter from Mgr. Heykamp, Old Catholic Bishop of Utrecht, urging him to break with the Episcopal Church. Further correspondence with the Bishop of Deventer convinced Vilatte that Utrecht valued him highly, and, if asked, might raise him to the episcopate. The thought proved to be too much for Father Vilatte and he began to seek the episcopate in earnest. When the matter came to the attention of Bishop Grafton of the Episcopal Church, he indicated to Utrecht that they could, if they choose, consecrate Vilatte, but he would then have to obtain his financial support from them.

Meanwhile, Vilatte was actively seeking someone (and it did not seem to matter who) to consecrate him a bishop. He approached Archbishop Vladimir, the Russian Orthodox Bishop of the Aleutian Islands, but did not meet with initial success. When word of this reached Bishop Grafton, he confronted Father Joseph and a fight soon broke out. Since Father Joseph had never taken an oath of obedience, he wasn't particularly inclined to be so. To emphasize his independence from the Episcopal

Bishop, he now opened a new mission station near Green Bay. Vilatte's hope of being consecrated by the Old Catholic Church of Europe began to evaporate. For a variety of reasons, the churches in Europe began to cool to this idea. Judging from the correspondence, they were not rejecting him personally; but as they grew closer to the Episcopal Church, it did not seem necessary to extend their jurisdiction to America. In any event, at the Old Catholic Congress in Cologne in 1890, the bishops decided not to consecrate Vilatte. Many writers looking back on the situation make the assumption that Father Joseph's erratic nature must have been apparent even across the miles of ocean, but the correspondence between Father Joseph and the Old Catholics of Europe gives no hint of this.

When the Old Catholics of Europe dropped their support of his cause, Father Joseph began to seek a new connection. He wanted to be a bishop and he wanted to be independent. Bishop Vladimir was willing to receive him as a priest, but had no inclination or authority to anything more. It was at this point that Father Vilatte began a correspondence with Mar Julius I, the Metropolitan of the Independent Catholic Church of Ceylon, Goa, and India. This church consisted of about 3,000 Catholics of the Latin Rite, and was in communion with the Syrian Jacobite Patriarch of Antioch, Ignatius Jacob II. The Patriarch had raised Julius Ferrette to the episcopate as Bishop of Iona in 1866, and he was presumably seeking ways to extend the influence of his small communion. In any event, both Bishop Alvarez (Mar Julius I) and his Patriarch responded favorably to Father Joseph's request for consecration.

The arguments that favored the consecration have a certain validity. It seemed that the struggling congregations in Wisconsin were either going to have to become merged with the Anglican Communion, or after Vilatte's death they would pass out of existence. Consequently, an informal synod was held and some $225 was raised by the Dyckesville parish. Father Vilatte immediately sailed for Ceylon where the consecration was to take place. Although the Patriarch and Bishop Alvarez were petitioned by Bishop Grafton not to proceed with the consecration, it took place on May 29, 1892. It cannot be said that the Church authorities in Antioch and India had too little time or opportunity to acquaint themselves with the facts in the case. Peter Anson suggests that Vilatte went to Ceylon lest Alvarez discover how few Americans desired to separate themselves from Rome. However, Bishop Grafton and others did everything possible to make these facts known. The mere fact that the petition to consecrate was only signed by one clergyman would have been sufficient to indicate to everyone that Father Joseph's following was small. Much has been made of the fact that the supporters of Vilatte were few and uneducated. The poverty of American Old Catholic bishops has been stressed in such a way as to imply that Holy poverty is reserved only for the lower clergy.

Bishop Vilatte returned to an admittedly small indigenous church. The chapel of St. Louis, at Green Bay, was raised to the status of a pro-cathedral, and two other churches remained under his jurisdiction, St. Joseph's at Walhain, and St. Mary's at Duval. The small diocese had a hard financial struggle, and the Bishop himself was frequently in debt. Whether for this reason or others, Bishop Vilatte carried on extensive negotiations with the Roman Church, attempting to find a basis for reunion. During this period he did not neglect his pastoral work, and found time to publish a prayer book and a catechism for the Old Catholics. Negotiations broke down, and Bishop Vilatte left Wisconsin in 1898, having turned over the care of the churches to Father Gauthier. Although Father Gauthier was sincere and capable, many of the people left to become Episcopalians or Roman Catholics, and some few joined a spiritual movement. The men who followed Father Gauthier, Fathers Lopez and Mouthy, were incapable and of low caliber and their work fell apart.

At this time a movement had begun among the Polish Catholics. Largely for ethnic reasons, there seemed to be great dissatisfaction with Roman Catholicism. In 1897 Father Antoni Kozlowski was consecrated by the Dutch Old Catholics. In many of the large Polish centers, priests and congregations separated themselves and formed independent Catholic Churches. In Buffalo, Stephen Kaminski, pastor of the Church of the Holy Mother of the Rosary, successfully appealed to Archbishop Vilatte (as he now called himself) to consecrate him. Unlike his work among the Belgians, this work was to last longer. However, it was left to others to continue. Bishop Kaminski had to flee his creditors and went to Canada for a short while, and when he returned, Archbishop Vilatte was not on the scene. However, he remained in charge of his parish until he died in 1911.

Many of the Polish Catholic Churches which were formed in the next half century were led by priests who had Old Catholic consecrations through Vilatte or through the Mathew succession. Many of them eventually found their way into the Polish National Catholic Church, of which we shall speak later. The remainder of Vilatte's life is a romantic and fascinating tale, but produced little or nothing that was constructive for Old Catholicism. He seems to have traveled extensively in Europe and America, ordaining priests and consecrating bishops. Few of these men ever succeeded in gathering a following or building churches.

One of the few consecrations that did result in something permanent was the consecration of George Alexander McGuire, as bishop of the African Orthodox Church. Shortly after this event, Bishop Vilatte traveled to his native France and returned to the Roman Catholic Church. Presumably he repented of his errant ways and acknowledged the authority of the Roman Pontiff. In any event, he was allowed to live at the Abbey of Pon-Colbert, a Cistercian Monastery near Versailles. Here he lived until his death on July 8, 1929.[21] According to Anson, a requiem Mass was celebrated as for a layman, and thus the man who would rival the Pope was buried without honors.

The Old Catholic Church, by Karl Prüter

IX.

CARMEL HENRY CARFORA
†

Carmel Henry Carfora was born in Italy, where he studied for the priesthood in the Roman Catholic Church. Upon the completion of his studies he was sent to North America to conduct missionary work among the Italian immigrants. He did not get along with his superiors, and, in a short time, broke away from Roman jurisdiction. He then proceeded to organize an independent Catholic mission among Italian immigrants in West Virginia.

It was inevitable that Father Carfora would encounter Bishop Paolo Miraglia-Culiotti, who headed the Italian National Episcopal Church. Bishop Paolo had been consecrated by Bishop Vilatte. For a while, Father Carfora and Bishop Paolo cooperated in ministering to Italian Americans, and in 1911 Paolo consecrated Carmel Henry Carfora as bishop. The new bishop did not want to serve in the Italian Episcopal Church, and instead organized in Ohio the National Catholic Diocese in North America. In the next few years Carfora traveled throughout the East and Midwest, and began to feel that he had a mission larger than the Italian-American community.

In 1916 another fortuitous meeting took place. This time he crossed paths with Bishop Prince de Landas Berghes et de Rache, who represented Arnold Harris Mathew of the Old Roman Catholic Church of England. At the time of the meeting Carfora had three small missions in West Virginia. We do not know why he decided to become part of the Old Roman Catholic Church, but he was reconsecrated by Bishop de Landas Berghes et de Rache, assisted by Bishop-Abbot Francis Brothers, on October 4, 1916. He was now bishop in the Old Roman Catholic Church of America, and was given the additional title of Archbishop of Canada.

The new archbishop began to attract thousands of widely scattered Italians, Poles, Lithuanians, and Ukrainians, plus a few Anglo-Saxon Americans. New congregations sprang up in almost every metropolitan center in the United States, although many lasted just for a short duration. Most were made up of dissatisfied Roman Catholics, although a number of Episcopalians joined the Old Roman Catholic Church. Among the latter were many clergymen who had doubts about Anglican Orders.

In spite of the fact that the Church was usually classified Old Catholic, there was little basis for doing so. Archbishop Carfora regarded himself as infallible, and the liturgy and the practices of the church were quite consistent with its title of "Old Roman" Catholic. In recent years, the Church has attempted to argue that Utrecht left the main stream of non-papal Catholicism when it recognized Anglican Orders.

The Church was beset by many internal problems, most of which seem to have been caused by the type of clergy it attracted. A large percentage of the clergymen were formerly dissatisfied Roman Catholics or Anglicans; if they had had problems in their former churches, they seem to have brought most of their problems into the new. Even as they had quarreled with their former bishops, so they quarreled with Archbishop Carfora. I have known priests who served under him, who said he was a kindly gentlemen, yet he deposed priests and bishops at an alarming rate. Most of those deposed went off to found new ecclesiastical bodies of their own.

For a while Archbishop Carfora joined with Archbishop Lloyd and the American Catholic Church, but the union was short lived. The two groups came together briefly in 1925, but by 1926 they went their separate ways once again. Old Catholicism in America has continued to be plagued with unity fever. Much time and effort that should go into the care and feeding of the flock has been expended in putting together one great American Old Catholic Church on paper. Hardly a month goes by without some new effort being made to unite all the Old Catholic Churches. Few succeed for any length of time. Since the 1960s, however, additional stable congregations have appeared, together with new jurisdictions and new bishops, and conceivably they might succeed where Carfora and others failed.

Carfora continued his efforts to expand the North American Old Roman Catholic Church, and even helped launch some new bodies in other parts of the world. On October 17, 1926,[22] he consecrated José Joachín Pérez y Budar as Archbishop of Mexico City. He was to head the Iglesia Ortodoxa Católica Mexicana, a group which had a promising mission field, but which never made much headway. However, the failure of this church or any of the other groups that were launched with Bishop Carfora's aid did not deter him from the practice of consecrating bishops indiscriminately. Many of these men remained with Bishop Carfora only a few months, and then went off to found new churches of their own. It seemed that almost any man could come to Bishop Carfora and hold out the hope that he could gather congregations from among his own particular ethnic group, and in return he would receive Episcopal consecration. It never seems to have occurred to Bishop Carfora, or any other Old Catholic for that matter, that it was possible for priests or laymen to do missionary work first, without becoming priests or bishops!

When Bishop Carfora died on January 11, 1958, his coadjutor, Cyrus A. Starkey, persuaded Bishop Richard A. Marchenna to accept the office of Supreme-Primate. The church, which never showed much cohesion at its best, now splintered into many factions. Among them was The North American Old Roman Catholic Church with Hubert A. Rogers as Primate, and the Old Roman Catholic Church in North America with Gerard George Shelley as Primate.

To add to the confusion of terms, the Diocese of Niagara Falls headed by Father Joseph Kelly had split from the North American Old Roman Catholic Church in 1951. It claimed to be the Old Roman Catholic Church in the U.S. and Canada, and to be in communion with Bishop Joseph Maria Thiesen, the Archbishop of the Old Roman Catholic Church of Germany. Archbishop Thiesen held orders in the Vilatte succession and so far as we can determine gathered no congregations in Germany. All of these groups managed to hold less than a dozen churches, although they usually had at least twice that number of clergymen, including bishops and archbishops.

THE OLD CATHOLIC CHURCH, BY KARL PRÜTER

X.

THE POLISH NATIONAL CATHOLIC CHURCH

✝

As we have seen in the chapter on Archbishop Joseph René Vilatte, the Poles in America came to him for help in establishing a free Catholic Church. The movement away from Rome among the Poles was due to a variety of factors. At first glance it would seem that the separation was a revival of the trustee dispute, since many of the arguments centered around the question of property ownership. In part it was a continuance of the ethnic quarrels that marked the colonial church. Both of these factors entered in, but the Polish quarrel was not a mere copy of the French and Irish disputes of an earlier period. The French and the Irish merely wanted a clergy of their own ethnic group, plus a say in the running of their church, or, at least, their own parishes. Much of the resentment directed towards the French bishops and priests was due to the fact that they did not seem American enough to suit their Irish and native-born parishioners. To the Irish, English with a French accent was resented, for the

Irishman was having difficulty in finding his place in America, even though he, unlike many other immigrants, spoke the language of the land.

The Pole, on the other hand, was not attempting to Americanize the church. On the contrary, he was anxious that it should be a bit of Poland on American soil. He wanted Polish priests, Polish customs, and above all the Polish language used in his church. In many American cities, the Poles like countless other immigrant groups had settled in the inner city and had established ethnic neighborhoods. One could work in a mill where Polish was spoken by most of the employees, shop in stores where the business was conducted in Polish, and chat with one's neighbors and friends in the Polish mother tongue. The church would, when a Polish priest was available, offer a sermon in that language. Unfortunately, Polish priests were not always available, and the Irish priests did not always suit their Polish parishioners.

Quarrels between people and clergy were frequent, and it is not surprising that some inevitably led to schism. Scranton, Pennsylvania had a large Polish population, and it was here that the Polish National Catholic Church (or PNCC) was born. Needless to say, the authorities in Rome were not happy to see the Old Trustee dispute coming to the surface again. In one Polish Roman Catholic Parish, the people and the priest quarreled. When they attempted to lock the pastor out of the church, the Roman authorities summoned the police. An unfortunate riot resulted and the people were determined to have control of their own church. However, they discovered that the deed to the church property was in the hands of the bishop, and that, without his sufferance, they were not the owners of the church building they had worked and paid for. Dismayed, they decided to start afresh and gather a new congregation and build a new church. They sought the advice and services of their former curate, Father Francis Hodur, who at this time was pastor of the Polish Roman Catholic parish of the Holy Trinity in nearby Nanticoke.[23] The people at Scranton were determined to have a priest of their own choosing and to own the church they built. Neither the congregation nor Father Hodur wished to break with Rome, and to that end Father Hodur went to Rome to present their case.

In a petition put before Rome, they voiced their desire to remain in communion with the church and set three conditions under which it would be possible. They wished that title to the church property be vested in the local parish church, that the parishes be free to choose Parish Committees, managerial and administrative, without interference on the part of priest or bishop and finally they wanted a voice in the assignment of parish priests.[24] Cardinal Ledochowski, who gave the official reply, left no door open to compromise. He reminded Father Hodur that the issue was presumably settled by the Synod of Baltimore in 1884.[25] What Cardinal Ledochowski overlooked was the fact that although the dispute was old and no new arguments were advanced, there was a new factor. The Poles were more determined than any other ethnic group to maintain their national heritage in America. Perhaps because there was no Polish nation, the Poles clung stubbornly to their traditions, their language, and their faith. It was

75

a saddened priest that returned to Scranton to report that Rome had read their petition but refused to make any concessions. The people of St. Stanislaus parish, at the meeting where the report was read, voted not to make any further appeals but to place their sole reliance upon God.

In few weeks' time, Father Hodur and his small flock were excommunicated from the Roman Church. The effect was electrifying and brought forth a variety of responses. Many Roman Catholics of Polish extraction avoided the independent church, but almost all the members responded by renewing their determination to go it alone. Very quickly they discovered that there were other groups of Poles in other communities that were anxious to have the same freedom. A group in Dickson City invited Father Hodur to come to them and explain the purpose and aims of "The Polish National Catholic Church," and on September 19, 1897, they organized themselves as St. Adelbert's Church. At this same meeting, Father Hodur assigned the Rev. Father Kławiter as its first priest.[26] The new group soon caught the imagination of Polish-Americans everywhere. In city after city, new parishes were organized. In some instances, the Roman priest took leadership, but usually it was the laity that took the first steps. In most cases the people had heard of the Polish National Catholic Church, and were planning to organize a congregation that would be part of that body.

By 1904 the churches under the PNCC banner met in a Synod at Scranton to elect their first bishop, The Rev. Father Francis Hodur. The new Church body was on the march, and it attracted the attention of Catholics throughout the nation. Once the idea of a Catholic church free of Rome was let lose upon the country, it took many forms. Among the Poles, many wished simply to organize independent parishes, while others identified themselves with the Old Catholic Church. One such group was organized in Chicago in 1895. Several parishes were formed and in 1897 Father Kozlowski was consecrated Bishop by the Old Catholic Church in Europe. In Cleveland, Ohio, and in Buffalo, New York, a similar group was formed in the same year. Unfortunately, in 1906 they elected as their bishop Father Kaminski, who proved to be unworthy. In 1913 Father Kaminski actually "sold" the property of the Buffalo parish to the Roman Diocese of Buffalo. As a result the church became involved in litigation, and the resulting scandal caused much disruption. This group in 1912 united with the Polish National Catholic Church. Throughout the country many independent groups sprang up. Some simply labeled themselves as independent Catholics, while others were attracted to the idea of calling themselves "Old Catholic." The group in Chicago did so because their orders came from the European Old Catholic Churches, the Buffalo group could claim orders from the Vilatte line, and others simply because it seemed like the best label to describe their faith and doctrines.

The Polish National Catholic Church was the body that seemed to attract most of the Polish congregations, and its growth, although, at first was slow, was steady. At the Second Synod of the Church in 1906, the Church placed tremendous power in the hands of the Bishop, and thereby insured stability that greatly aided in its growth. It also directed a committee to translate the liturgy from Latin into Polish.[27] This step was a tremendous factor in stimulating the growth of the church among the many millions living in America for whom Polish was the mother tongue. Unfortunately, no thought was given, at this time, to the translation of the Mass into English, and when the time came that English became the language of their people, the Polish National Church was slow in adopting it.

By 1919 it was felt that the time had come to plant missions in the Polish homeland. Father Bronislaw Krupski was sent as the first emissary. He was warmly welcomed in Poland, and after a brief lecture tour asked Bishop Hodur to join him. The start in Poland proved to be as stormy as that in America. Many Roman Catholics did much to make life difficult for the new church, and clashes with the local and national authorities were frequent. In spite of, or perhaps because of, persecution, the Church in Poland grew and prospered. By 1939 the Church claimed a membership of approximately 400,000 souls.[28] In the early 1970s the Church claimed to have 160 parishes in the United States and Canada. They also claimed a quarter of a million members. That, of course, would mean that the average parish had over 1,500 members, but I doubt if there was a single PNCC parish that had anywhere near that number.

The future of this church is very uncertain at the present time because of its ethnic orientation. Fortunately, many parishes have tried to move with the times. Since the use of Polish has declined in many of its parishes, English masses have been instituted. Nevertheless, the parishes continue to be ethnic Polish parishes. A friend of the author who serves as priest in one parish tells him that every sermon must end by calling the people to remain faithful, "To God, to country, and to Poland!"

In matters of faith the church has adhered to its Catholic origins, and there has been surprisingly little change from the Roman Catholic position. Attempts have been made by its opponents to suggest great and sweeping changes in the direction of Protestantism. One of these is the elevation of the preaching of the gospel to the status of a Sacrament, and another is Hodur's rejection of an eternal hell. To Bishop Hodur's mind, the idea of a hell inflicting eternal torture upon any of God's children seemed inconsistent with the love of Jesus Christ.[29]

In the light of the revolution in the Roman Church today these changes seem slight. Perhaps what the critics feared was that any change, however slight, would eventually bring the Polish National Church closer to Protestantism. Currently in the PNCC there is a strong Hodurite faction, which not only supports Hodur's doctrinal ideas, but also has continued to fight any effort to drop the word "Polish" from its name or to move the church away from its ethnic character. The latter has been a major factor in its continued decline over the last few decades. Today, it has fewer than 14,000 members in 144 parishes in the United States and Canada. To serve these parishes the Polish National Catholic Church has recruited dedicated priests willing to serve at very small salaries. The church has difficulty in finding sufficient clergy and recruits many from other denominations. It currently is talking with both the Roman Catholic Church and the Antiochian Church concerning possible union. In view of the fact that neither of these communions accept married bishops, it seems unlikely that these talks will result in a union.

XI.

THE AFRICAN ORTHODOX CHURCH
✝

It is a paradox that the Americanization of the Church brought into being a number of distinctly ethnic churches.

But after the turn of the century few ethnic groups were content to accept the leadership of the sons of dissimilar ethnic groups which had preceded them to these shores. The Blacks, particularly from the West Indies, were no longer content to be led by white bishops. In 1921, Dr. George Alexander McGuire, an Episcopal priest, left that church to establish the Independent Episcopal Church.

Father McGuire, who was then fifty-five years of age, had had a distinguished career in the Episcopal Church. He had served parishes both in the United States and in Antigua. At one time, he was considered for the post of Suffragan Bishop of Arkansas, but declined in order to study medicine at Jefferson Medical College, where he graduated as a Doctor of Medicine in 1910. After leaving Arkansas, he worked at St. Bartholomew's Episcopal Church in Cambridge, Massachusetts. After six

81

years of successful labor in that parish, he was called by Bishop Green, Bishop of New York, to be the Secretary of the Commission for Work Among the Colored People under the Board of Missions of the Protestant Episcopal Church. This gave him opportunities to travel on behalf of the Mission Board, and he became well known among the Episcopal clergy throughout the country.

His next call took him to the island of his birth, Antigua. Here he remained for six years building the church where he was baptized, St. Paul's in Sweets. When the movement of the "United Negro Improvement Association of the World" was formed under the leadership of a fellow West Indian, Marcus Garvey, Father McGuire returned to the United States in order to give Garvey support.

The idea of serving in a church where few Negroes were in positions of leadership had grown distasteful to him, and he was determined to pursue an independent course. On September 2, 1921, in the Church of the Good Shepherd in New York City, a meeting was held of all the Independent Episcopal ministers. The meeting resolved itself into the First Synod of the African Orthodox Church, and elected Dr. George Alexander McGuire to be its first bishop. The Synod then entered into negotiations with the American Catholic Church, headed by Archbishop Joseph René Vilatte, in order to secure valid orders for the bishop-elect. On September 28, 1921, Bishops Vilatte and Carl Nybledh consecrated Dr. McGuire in the Church of Our Lady of Good Death in Chicago.

A summary of the proceedings of the first General Synod reveals that Archbishop Vilatte and his group were not the first choice of the Synod. They were interested in a close relationship with the Eastern Orthodox Churches, but such a relationship was incompatible with their desire to pursue an independent course. None of the Orthodox Churches with whom they were in touch were willing to consecrate Father McGuire if the group was unwilling to be a part of their communion.

The Church experienced slow but steady growth, although most of the individual congregations were small. The priests were seldom able to devote full time to their charges, although every church was encouraged to contribute something to their support. The Endich Theological Seminary was organized for the training of the clergy, and the first class numbered fourteen men. The school was located on Long Island and provided about a year of training for its students. Because of the low educational level of its applicants, the school never evolved into a degree-granting accredited institution. It did, however, provide a minimal training for the clergy, and served as a screening agent for the church's candidates for Holy Orders. Because of a lack of sufficient candidates, it was forced to close in the early 1970s and the church, like most Old Catholic jurisdictions, has to rely on the institutions of other denominations for the training of its clergy.

During his lifetime Archbishop McGuire remained at the head of the church, and it enjoyed peace and stability. After his death in 1934, the leadership of the church fell into the less able hands of Archbishop W. E. J. Robertson. Shortly after his elevation to the Archbishopric, dissatisfaction arose among some of the clergy. According to Father

Terry-Thompson, the leader of the dissidents was the Rt. Rev. Richard Grant Barrow. The Communion was now divided with two groups claiming to be "The African Orthodox Church." The issue was finally taken into court, and under the leadership of Archbishop Robertson, the group was granted the use of the name African Orthodox Church.

The two groups continued their separate existence until shortly before the death of Archbishop Robertson. Then in 1965, under the leadership of Bishop Gladston St. Clair Nurse, the Barrow group agreed to re-unite with the parent body. Upon Archbishop Robertson's death, the reunited African Orthodox Church elected Bishop Nurse to become the third Archbishop of the Church. By this time the Church had become a world church with congregations in the United States and Canada, together with congregations in the West Indies and on the Continent of Africa.

Upon Archbishop Nurse's death in 1976, William Russell Miller was elected to succeed him. Archbishop Miller managed to hold the united Church together, but after his resignation in 1981, the church once more fractured. The synod which met at Chicago elected Bishop Stafford James Sweeting as the new Archbishop. The Church went along for only a few months under Archbishop Sweeting's leadership, when Archbishop G. Duncan Hinkson of St. Augustine's Church in Chicago withdrew to form the African Orthodox Church of the West. This Western jurisdiction managed to add two new parishes, one in Houston, Texas, and one in San Francisco. The latter is served by Bishop Franzo King.

In 1995 history was destined to repeat itself. Once again the fractured Church was able to reunite. Archbishop Hinkson worked tirelessly to do so, and at a joint synod held at St. Augustine Cathedral in Chicago on January 29th of that year, the union was accomplished. The Most Rev. James Bernardt Butler was elected Primate Metropolitan, with Archbishop Duncan Hinkson Primate Co-Adjutor. The newly united Church has seventeen parishes throughout the United States and approximately 2,500 members.

In 2004 Bishop Hinkson died, and has been succeeded by Archbishop Jamen Butler. Doctor Hinkson will be remembered along with Dr. George Alexander McGuire and Gladstone St. Clair Nurse as having built the church and preserved its unity for over half a century.

THE OLD CATHOLIC CHURCH, BY KARL PRÜTER

XII.

THE FREE CATHOLIC MOVEMENT
†

In the 1930s Old Catholics began to do work among the Congregational Christian Churches, with surprising success and long-range effects. At first glance, this would have seemed an unlikely field for Old Catholic missionary efforts. But to those familiar with Congregational history, it was less of an evangelistic effort than a call to return to the catholic heritage of the Pilgrim Fathers.

The early Congregationalists were Christocentric, and their worship centered around the Blessed Sacrament. Their devotion to the Sacrament grew directly out of the fact that it had been specifically commanded by our Lord Jesus Christ. In fact, their entire church life was a simple attempt to put into effect what Christ willed for them as individuals and as a congregation. However, without the episcopacy they quickly fell away from their Catholic doctrine and practices. In the early nineteenth century, the Unitarian Movement had made deep inroads into Congregationalism; before the end of the century, almost every vestige of Catholicism had disappeared.

It was the early meetings of the Ecumenical Movement that sparked the revival of the Catholic heritage in Congregationalism. The publication of the General Council's *Book of Worship for Free Churches* and Karl Prüter's *A Divine Liturgy for Free Churches* pointed the way toward Catholic revival. A small but significant number of churches began to celebrate Mass on a weekly basis using either *The Divine Liturgy for Free Churches*, the Anglican *Book of Common Prayer*, or *The Old Catholic Missal and Liturgy* edited by Archbishop Mathew and Archbishop Gul in 1909.

Orders also became a matter of concern. A few ministers sought and received Catholic ordinations from American Old Catholic bishops. Bishop Howard Mather served the Order of Antioch while functioning as a Congregational pastor in a number of Congregational Churches, including the historic Church at Sheffield, Massachusetts. Often they met with serious opposition, but in most instances the congregations regarded what was happening as a revival of true Congregationalism. Those in the Liturgical Movement had considerable support from influential persons in the Congregational Churches. Dr. Raymond Calkins led the way by affirming a faith in the Real Presence, and Dr. Douglas Horton, father of the United Church of Christ, gave encouragement to the small group of Free Catholics who appeared across the country in such places as Pittsburgh, PA, Tarentum, PA, Sheffield, MA, Orford, NH, Chicago, IL, Berwyn, IL, Belchertown, MA,

México, D.F., México, Champaign, IL, and Philadelphia, PA.

The movement was just gathering momentum when Congregationalism was dealt a shattering blow. The merger, which was vigorously fought by a small group of dedicated souls, was finally consummated with the Evangelical and Reformed Church. The United Church of Christ was formed for the avowed purpose of reducing the number of denominations in the country. Like many similar attempts before it, the result was a net increase. Whereas before there had been two denominations, there now emerged five. Most of the Congregational Churches became part of the new United Church, but large numbers, including many that were labeled as "Free Catholic," regrouped in new ecclesiastical bodies. The following groups attempted, each in its own way, to preserve the heritage: The Conservative Congregational Conference, The Midwest Congregational Christian Fellowship, The National Association of Congregational Christian Churches, and Christ Catholic Church.

The latter Communion was formed in 1965, when leaders of the Free Catholic Movement became concerned that it was going to become another victim of the merger. The Rev. Hugo R. Prüter, who had been pastor of the North Berwyn Congregational Church, attempted to preserve the Catholic heritage in that church, first through affiliation with the National Association, and then through affiliation with the Midwest Congregational Fellowship. However, none of the other members of these associations seemed interested in preserving Catholicism, even those which had been a part of the

Free Catholic Movement. They felt their very existence was at stake, and they seemed not to care about the nature of that existence.

The Rev. Prüter worked for a while with the Pilgrim Missionary Society, and even attempted a new Catholic mission in Itasca, Illinois. A church was organized, but the members who flocked to the Congregational banner were not Catholic in thought or practice. Realizing that with the existing organizations Free Catholic parishes were not possible, The Rev. Prüter resigned from his parish in 1965 and made a pilgrimage to Europe.

After visiting several Old Catholic Churches, and after much thought, he went to a small chapel in Upper Bavaria at Traunwallchen and there he sought for direction. He returned to the States in 1965 with the burning conviction that he would find a Catholic parish which would satisfy his spiritual needs. He settled in Boston in order to do some graduate study, and here he began his search for a Free Catholic parish. Since there was none to be found, he visited Archbishop Peter A. Zhurawetzky of Christ Catholic Church of the Americas and Europe and placed the problem before him. He received Catholic orders and the religious name of Father Karl, and with Archbishop Peter's blessing organized a parish in Boston's Back Bay area. Two years later, at Archbishop Peter's request, Father Karl was consecrated bishop. In 1968 the Diocese of Boston was designated an independent autonomous Communion, free to carry on its Old Catholic and Free Catholic traditions as Christ Catholic Church, Diocese of Boston.

What the new Church sought to preserve is the basic tenets and teachings of our Lord Jesus Christ and the Church and the Sacraments which he gave us. Some continuing Congregationalists may find the role of the bishop and the method of property ownership objectionable. Christ Catholics would reply that the early church had bishops, and that the property of the church belongs neither to the bishop nor to the congregation, but to Christ, who is the head of every church. In few churches of any tradition is there this sense of trusteeship. All too often congregations believe *they* own the property and that *they* may govern the church as they please. A Congregational historian, Dale, insisted that congregations are free only to worship as Christ directs them, to call as their pastor only those men whom Christ has chosen for them, and to preach those doctrines which Christ has given them. Christ Catholic Church claims that it follows no church order nor preaches any doctrine except that which has been given to us by Jesus Christ and handed down by the Apostles. It sees its mission to seek out people not because they wish to be Catholics or Congregationalists, or anything else, but solely on the basis of their willingness to follow Jesus Christ.

XIII.

CHRIST CATHOLIC CHURCH
✝

In the early nineteen hundreds there was a wave of new immigrants settling in America and attempting to adjust to a new life. Many were Roman Catholic Poles, Lithuanians, Czechs, and Germans who had difficulty adapting themselves to the ways of the Irish clergy. In addition, a new sense of independence manifested itself, and many of the immigrants wanted to throw off the traditional discipline of the Roman Church. One would have difficulty finding the motives which produced the restlessness among the immigrants, for they were many and varied.

In the first part of the twentieth century, the American Catholic Church experienced innumerable schisms, both small and large. The largest was the formation of the Polish National Catholic Church, but more often it was an isolated family or individual that drifted away. Many of the latter found their way into or helped form independent Orthodox and Catholic Churches. When whole congregations and their priests broke away, they usually sought to have the priest ordained by someone in the Villate or Mathew line of succession, and proceeded to establish a new church.

In 1937 a number of churches of Slavic background came together and formed the Polish Old Catholic Church. They incorporated in New Jersey and elected Father Joseph Zielonka as their first bishop. Most of these churches were in New Jersey in such places as New Brunswick, South River, Dover, and Dunnellen, although they were represented in Springfield, Massachusetts, and Philadelphia, Pennsylvania. The Church grew steadily and by 1960 consisted of thirty-two parishes and approximately 7,200 members.

Upon the death of, by then, Archbishop Zielonka in 1961, his Suffragan Bishop, Peter A. Zhurawetsky, was raised to the office of Archbishop. Bishop Peter had been consecrated at Springfield, Massachusetts in 1950 by Patriarch Joseph Klimovicz of the Orthodox Catholic Patriarchate of America, assisted by Archbishop Konstantine Jaroshevich, a Byelorussian Prelate who had been consecrated by Archbishop Fan Stylin Noli of the Albanian Orthodox Church, Archbishop Zielonka, Metropolitan Nicholas Bohatyretz of the Ukrainian Church, and Old Catholic Bishop Peter M. Williamowicz.

In the same year, in order to lift barriers so that all nationalities might feel welcome, the Church changed its name to Christ Catholic Church of the Americas and Europe. The future looked good and the fields seemed ripe for the harvest, but a number of problems began to plague the small polygot Church. First, not all of the churches and clergy were willing to accept the leadership of the new Archbishop, Peter A. Zhurawetzky. Second, Father Felix Starazewski was regarded by many as the legitimate successor of Bishop Zielonka. He and his parish in South River, New Jersey, would not accept the jurisdiction of Archbishop Peter. The third and perhaps most critical factor was the attempt to form a union with other Old Catholic and Orthodox bodies. The internecine quarrels which characterized so much of the free catholic movement of this period, not only affected the cooperative synods, but also spilled over into Christ Catholic Church and splintered it. By 1965 the church had been reduced to a handful of communicants and clergy.

At this time the church began to receive strength from several new sources. The Church of the Transfiguration was organized in Boston and the Church of St. Paul was organized in Hobbs, New Mexico. These parishes were made up of new converts from Roman Catholic and Episcopal churches, and consisted of people who had no intention or desire to continue quarrels of the past decade. Further, the clerical leadership now consisted of men for whom loyalty to the archbishopric was viewed as necessary to good church order.

In 1967, the Diocese of Boston was established and in the same year the Diocese of New Mexico and the East. For a few years, Bishop Daniel Smith carried on active work in Hobbs, New Mexico, but later moved to Denver, where he served the Church of St. Paul.

In 1969, the Monastery of Our Lady of Reconciliation was established at Glorietta, New Mexico. Here under the leadership of Bishop Christopher

95

William Jones, as Abbot, the monastery ministered to many of the disenchanted youth of the sixties. Bishop Jones wrote such books as *Listen Pilgrim* and *Look Around, Pilgrim.*

Archbishop Peter was less interested in this new growth than in his desire to build an American Patriarchate. So in 1967 when two parishes in Boston, Massachusetts and Deering, New Hampshire served by Father Karl Prüter, who was to be consecrated bishop, requested that they be designated as an autocephalous jurisdiction, Archbishop Peter readily agreed. The new jurisdiction, Christ Catholic Church, Diocese of Boston, was very quickly shaped by Bishop Karl Prüter's experience with the Free Catholic Movement.

The new church body grew quickly, and when in 1979 it gathered in Chicago, clergy and laity came from parishes in Maine, Illinois, Rhode Island, and Massachusetts. In addition there were proxy votes from parishes in Arizona and New Mexico. St. Willibrord Press had published such books and pamphlets as *A History of the Old Catholic Church*, *The Teachings of the Great Mystics*, "The House Church Movement," and "Are You a Catholic Without Knowing It?" More important, it had become the leading distributor of books and pamphlets in the Orthodox and Catholic Autocephalous Movement. Not only did it handle the books of Bishops Prüter and Jones, but books by other Old Catholics, and even some by the opponents of the movement such as Peter Anson, C. B. Moss, and Henry Brandreth. If you wanted books about Old Catholicism, the obvious source for scholars, students of the movement, and the curious was St. Willibrord Press.

At Chicago the synod also dropped the designation of "Diocese of Boston" and assumed the name Christ Catholic Church, for all the parishes using that name were now members of the Holy Synod. The Church seemed to be on the march and Bishop Prüter made a move to Missouri, where he built The Cathedral of the Prince of Peace, which was soon listed in the *Guinness Book of World Records* as the world's smallest Cathedral.

A year later, Father Philip Avila Oliver was consecrated as Bishop of the Northeast at St. Augustine's Cathedral in Chicago by Bishop Karl Prüter, assisted by Archbishop G. Duncan Hinkson and Bishop Jean LaPointe.

A new period of growth began, and new parishes were added in such places as Deming, Columbus, Las Cruces, New Mexico, and Le Roy, Illinois. At the same time, the church began to consider merger with the Ontario Old Roman Catholic Church of Canada. In 1989 Bishop Prüter consecrated Father Frederick Dunleavy as Archbishop. A union between the two jurisdictions was formed, largely on mutual faith, with few written documents. Bishop Karl Prüter was accepted as Presiding Bishop, although there was never a formal vote. About this time a Macedonian Call came from Salt Lake City. A small Old Catholic parish had been gathered by Bishop Raymond Sawyer, who had been consecrated a year earlier by Bishop Andrew Barbeau of the Charismatic Catholic Church. The parish had over seventy-five members and had been renting a church building which the owners had just sold to another congregation. Things began to unravel and Bishop Sawyer and his three priests asked to come into Christ Catholic Church. Bishop Sawyer agreed to serve as a priest but later left Salt Lake City and went out on his own. One of the priests, Father W. Wolfgang Gossett, moved to Newport, Oregon, where in time he gathered St. Barnabas Christ Catholic Mission. The Salt Lake City parish scattered, although Father Robert Meredith attempted to regather the parish.

In 1989 the Church met in Synod at Republic, Missouri. Bishop Prüter resigned as Presiding Bishop, and Archbishop Dunleavy was elected as Presiding Bishop with the title of Archbishop. The formal elevation took place on June 18, 1982, and at that time Archbishop Frederick Dunleavy suggested to Bishop Prüter that the Church enter into negotiations with the Liberal Catholic Church of Ontario, since it seemed that the two bodies had enough in common that they ought to unite. A joint synod was arranged at Niagara Falls, Canada, in June of 1993, and the delegates voted to affirm the merger and the election of Archbishop W. Donald Mullan as Presiding Bishop. It was also agreed that the name of the joint Church should be Christ Catholic Church. Perhaps because this was the only significant change for the Liberal Catholic Church, there was little opposition to the name change, and the vote in favor was overwhelming. Actually, there was only one negative vote, and it was later revealed that the priest who cast it held theosophical views. This was soon to prove a problem to the new Church. When the new church was chartered in Canada it took the name of Christ Catholic Church International.

The merger lasted just three years, for it soon was discovered that the two groups did not have a common understanding of what it means to be Catholic. After much discussion and hard labor to develop a Constitution, Catechism, and Statement of Faith it became apparent that the differences ran very deep. The united Church had adopted as a common statement of faith, Archbishop Mathew's Declaration of Union, and it was hoped that this would eliminate many of the problems. However, it was in the area of practice where a wide fissure developed. In Christ Catholic Church the parishes either used the Christ Catholic Mass or the Tridentine Mass. A few used the Liturgy of St. John Chrysostom. The Constitution, before the merger, had specified that only the Christ Catholic Mass or one of the traditional and historic liturgies could be used. Those parishes coming from the Liberal Catholic Church had been used to a cafeteria style approach to liturgy as well as theology. Most used a liturgy called "The St. Francis Liturgy," which was eclectic and varied from parish to parish. There were also elements of the liturgy which were copied from the *Novus Ordo*, which traditional Catholics find objectionable. Most of the hymns used at the Cathedral Church at Niagara Falls came from Protestantism and are fundamentalist and Pentecostal; for example, applause was frequently heard during even the most solemn and sacred portions of the Holy Mass.

Naturally, with these views the leadership in Canada took an ecumenical direction and brought the church into communion with a number of unorthodox bodies, including The Federation of Independent Catholic Churches. With the revelation of the latter action, Archbishop Karl called for the dissolution of the merger.

Christ Catholic Church now consists of six parishes in the United States and one each in Canada and Australia. At the center is the Cathedral of the Prince of Peace and the Garden of Saints at Highlandville, Missouri which attract thousands of visitors annually. The Cathedral Bookstore continues to supply books and other material for the entire Independent Catholic and Orthodox Movement. Archbishop Karl is currently writing a *History of War and Peace.*.

The Archbishop says that "Future growth of the church will come one soul and one parish at a time. It will come because we have taken an uncompromising stand for the traditional Old Catholic Faith."

XIV.

CHRIST CATHOLIC
CHURCH INTERNATIONAL
†

This Church owes its name to a short-lived merger with Christ Catholic Church. It began as the Liberal Catholic Church of Ontario and its history goes back to the 1930s, when the Rev. W. Harry Daw left the Anglican priesthood to organize an Old Catholic parish in Hamilton, Ontario. The new parish, St. Francis of Assisi, grew rapidly, and sent a signal that many people in Ontario would welcome an Old Catholic Church that was traditional in faith, and yet innovative in its outreach. The parish was much alone and welcomed the friendship of the Bishop Charles Hampton of the Liberal Catholic Church International. Although St. Francis did not share the theosophical views of the Liberal Catholics, they entered into communion in order to end their isolation.

In the early 1950s Father Daw led the group into the Liberal Catholic Church faction under Bishop Edward Murray Matthews. He was consecrated by Matthews on October 2, 1955, taking the position of the first Bishop of the Liberal Catholic Church of

Ontario. He held this position until 1974, resigning in favor of John Henry Russell, who served as Presiding Bishop until 1985.

The Church then entered into a period of expansion beyond Hamilton, appointing a former Lutheran pastor, Father Del Baier to open a mission in Brantford, Ontario. Later, Bishop Russell ordained a former Anglican, William Donald Mullan, to the priesthood at Blessed Trinity Church on April 2, 1978, and authorized him to open a mission in Niagara Falls. St. Francis Church began one week later, and today occupies its own building in Chippawa, a suburb of Niagara Falls. Father Mullan very quickly began two other new works. He began to celebrate a weekly Mass at the Niagara Falls Campground, and attracted so many people that a chapel was built and dedicated to St. Francis. He also gathered a second parish in Niagara Falls, St. Luke's, for which he bought a wooden structure in the Town of Stamford. The congregation was housed there until the present building on Palmer Avenue was purchased from the Roman Catholic Church.

The new building was acquired because the Social Planning Council of Niagara Falls said that the area's greatest need was for emergency accommodation for homeless boys. St. Luke's was quick to accept the challenge and make the necessary financial sacrifices to turn an empty school house into a home for boys on the second floor, and to provide new quarters for the church on the ground floor. The Holy Family Boys Home opened in December of 1982, and over the years has housed some seven hundred youngsters who needed a place to stay, either for one night, or for an extensive residency.

At the death of Bishop John Henry Russell in 1985, his co-adjutor, Bishop Thomas McCourt, took the helm. Bishop McCourt began an immediate reorganization in order to meet the needs of the growing church. On August 10, 1986, he consecrated Father William Donald Mullan bishop. The co-consecrators were Bishops Harry Daw and Illtyd Thomas. The latter was from the Celtic Catholic Church.

Later in the year the parish council of Blessed Trinity, which was served by Bishop McCourt, voted to close. Bishop McCourt felt that since most of the activity within the church now centered in Niagara Falls that he would resign as Presiding Bishop. The synod then elected Bishop Mullan to succeed him. Under Bishop Mullan the church rapidly expanded to other communities. The Bishop called Father Larry Whissell from British Columbia to begin a new mission in Metro Toronto. Father Whissell responded by opening St. Jude's parish in Etobicoke in 1987 and St. Bridget's Church in Toronto in 1990. Another parish, St. Cuthbert's, was opened in Oakville by Father Arthur Keating in 1989.

In 1990 it was decided that an auxiliary bishop was needed, and Father John Brown was consecrated by Archbishop Dean Bekken of the Liberal Catholic Church International. He was assisted by another LCCI bishop, The Rt. Rev. John Jenkins, and Archbishop Mullan. The assistance of LCCI Bishop Joseph Demers was sought to be pastor of St. Jude's, and to serve as bishop of the New Diocese of Toronto and St. Cuthbert's, in Mississauga Oakville. Bishop Demers ran into solid opposition

103

in the LCCO, when he started publicly to unveil his theosophical leanings, and the LCCI ruled that clergy must be allowed to express their own thoughts as long as they point out that their beliefs do not reflect the official teaching of the Church, and the Liberal Catholic Church of Ontario should not do otherwise. The LCCO immediately took action and voted in February of 1991 to "put on hold" affiliation with the LCCI until such time as they produced an official statement of beliefs, in order to enforce the LCCO Statement of Orthodox Catholic beliefs. This action prompted Bishop Demers and an associate to walk out, resigning posts with the LCCO, and maintaining ties with the LCCI. He expected most of the Diocese of Toronto would leave with him, but all churches in the Diocese remained loyal to the Ontario Church and Bishop Demers moved back to the United States.

The Church having severed ties with the LCCI, it began to move forward and expanded by adding missions in Ottawa in 1991, Scarborough, Windsor, and St. Catherines in 1993. Other missions were established earlier in Winnipeg, Manitoba, Hamilton, Ontario, and South Hero, Vermont. In addition the Church became actively involved in chaplaincy in hospitals, nursing homes, senior citizen's homes, and to veterans' organizations. It began an annual summer camp for underprivileged youngsters and a food and clothing depot for needy people.

About this time the Church received overtures from Archbishop Frederick Dunleavy of Christ Catholic Church to enter into union negotiations. On the surface it seemed as if the two denominations had much in common. Archbishop Mullan and

Archbishop Dunleavy began the discussions, but toward the end of the negotiations Archbishop Dunleavy turned over the proceedings to Bishop Prüter, and an agreement to unite was soon reached. Archbishop W. Donald Mullan became the Presiding Bishop of Christ Catholic Church International. The Bishop W. H. Daw Seminary was officially recognized as the Church's institution for the training of its clergy in an effort to provide resident, as well as extension programs for the entire church.

However, both parties to the union soon discovered how far apart they were in theology, but more especially in practice. *The St. Luke Magazine* carried articles and photos which proved to be a constant irritant to most of the parishes south of the border. News of weddings on base ball diamonds, and misprints which suggested the Bishop Daw Seminary would train women to be ordained as deaconesses, and a letter from a deacon in the Canadian Church who was clearly pro-choice on the abortion question, brought scores of protests. The dissent from south of the Border seemed to drive Bishop Mullan to accelerate his ecumenical activities. 1995 was a year in which the church completed two mergers and reached out in new and more liberal directions. Several priests were received from the former Mercian Orthodox Catholic Church, and soon four of them were consecrated as bishops. A second union was brought about by the reception of the Old Catholic Church of British Columbia and its bishop, The Most Rev. J. Gerard Laplante. It brought into the Church St. Raphael's Old Catholic Church, which has a quaint and quite attractive church edifice in Vancouver.

A concordat was reached with the Free Greek Orthodox Church under Bishop M. S. Melchizek. As part of the agreement the Bishop Daw Seminary was absorbed by the St. Elias Orthodox Catholic Seminary. The Seminary is now located both in Niagara Falls and Lincoln, Nebraska. Another concordat was reached with the Holy Eastern Orthodox Catholic and Apostolic Church in North America headed by The Most Reverend Wolodymyr II. In its desire for ecumenical relations, the church joined the Fellowship of Independent Catholic and Orthodox Bishops under the leadership of Matriarch Meri Louise Spruit. Shortly after joining, Archbishop Mullan withdrew, stating that he had not fully understood the aims and goals of the group.

It is not clear where all these various ecumenical endeavors will take Christ Catholic Church International. It is managing to add many names to its roster of priests and now has almost as many parishes in the United States as in Canada. The Church now has a distinctly liberal flavor, and resembles the modern Roman Church more than it does traditional Old Catholicism. Not surprisingly, it has attracted several former Roman Catholic priests, and one of them serves the largest parish in CCC International. Archbishop Mullan definitely wishes to see the church grow faster than "at one soul and one parish at a time."

XV.

OTHER OLD CATHOLIC
BODIES IN AMERICA
†

Today there are more than two hundred Old Catholic jurisdictions in North America. The largest of those, except for those we have previously discussed, has about two dozen parishes. They are hard to track because they frequently disappear or merge with other jurisdictions, and also because new jurisdictions are organized almost every month. Some do not survive the year, but many do. It has to be remembered that Old Catholic do not have old and endowed missionary societies which can support a new and struggling mission. Most of the Old Catholic missions get their start as a result of the work of a dedicated priest. He is almost always the principle contributor. I discovered when one of my priests died that he never permitted an offering to be taken during one of his Masses. Fortunately, he had the free use of a chapel, but the candles, the wine, the communion bread, the Mass booklets, in fact everything the parish needed, he paid out of his own pocket.

While he lived he had a regular attendance of about twenty-five people, but when he died, although they revered him, few were ready to take on the responsibilities of church membership, and the parish ceased to function. This is not an isolated case, and unfortunately, many bishops and priests continue to subsidize their parishes. As a consequence, too many parishes fail to survive the loss of their clergy. The one reason Old Catholicism continues to grow is the fact that there are so many clergy willing to freely give their time and labor, and from their efforts new missions spring up across the nation almost every week.

One of the most active and viable groups is The Old Roman Catholic Church in North America, under the leadership of Bishop Francis P. Facione. The Church has few actual parishes, but claims a membership of approximately 4,000. Its quarterly magazine, *New Perspectives*, is well written in an attractive format.

Another small but viable group is The Old Roman Catholic Church, under James Edward Bostwick. It was founded by the late Bishop Walter X. Brown. With less than ten parishes, it managed for many years to maintain a home for homeless boys and a separate establishment for recovering alcoholics. A decade ago it gave up the homes in order to expand its parish ministry. The Church is based in Oconomowoc, Wisconsin.

One of the fastest growing jurisdictions is The American Catholic Church under Bishop Peter Hickman. A few decades before the Episcopal Church gave us a bishop living with a male lover, The American Catholic Church declared "same sex" marriages to be both normal and moral. Since then the word "inclusive" is being used by many Old Catholic jurisdictions, as well as many mainline churches. Unfortunately, many of Old Catholic organizationns came into being precisely because the mainline churches were firm in holding to traditional Christian morality. Now that there is confusion in almost all of the churches, it is doubtful if a new Old Catholic jurisdiction built solely on the idea of being all-inclusive will be created. has about a half dozen parishes from California to Pennsylvania.

There are over five hundred bishops who claim to be a part of the Autocephalous Church of the Apostolic Succession. They call themselves Anglican, Old Catholic, Traditional Catholic, or Orthodox. For the most part they have few parishes. Most have only one parish. A number of the Traditional Catholic priests are under no bishop at all, and serve no particular parish, but go from house chapel to chapel, much as did the old Methodist circuit riders in early America. Whether Old Catholic, Traditional Catholic, or Orthodox, their growth has been phenomenal. It is the writer's opinion that the development of new jurisdictions has peaked, and that future growth will be in the expansion of some of the existing Churches, such as the North American Old Roman Catholic Church in North America and Christ Catholic Church.

Many of the independents, particularly the Anglicans and the Traditionalists, look to further defections from the Episcopal Church and the Roman Church to aid in their growth. I believe they seek in vain. Any Episcopalian who can tolerate the acceptance by the entire Church of Bishop Gene Robinson of the Diocese of Vermont, will accept any further changes that might come to the Episcopal Church. And believe me, there is more to come.

The Roman Catholic Church, on the other hand, shows no new signs of further erosion of faith and doctrine. Some American Roman Catholics will continue to agitate for female priests, the acceptance of homosexuality, and birth control, but are prepared to accept the Pope's unwillingness to change his views on these matters. The question of birth control, like Papal Infallibility, has already been settled by most Catholics. They practice birth control because they know the Pope is not infallible. In all other matters, however, they follow the Pope and give him due reverence and fealty. The Traditionalists will not grow because there are no longer many Catholics who even remember, let alone have any nostalgia for, the old Latin Mass.

The main factors that will fuel the growth of the Autocephalous Churches will continue to be their ability to evangelize the unchurched, and their attraction to Protestants who are seeking a fuller sacramental and liturgical expression of their faith than is offered by any of the churches they now attend.

NOTES
✝

[1]Moss, C. B. *The Old Catholic Movement, Its Origins and History, Second Edition.* New York: Morehouse-Barlow Co., 1966, p. 101-103.

[2]*Ibid.*, p. 117.

[3]*Ibid.*, p. 122-123.

[4]*Ibid.*, p. 202-203.

[5]*Ibid.*, p. 202-203.

[6]Walker, Williston. *A History of the Christian Church.* New York: Charles Scibner's Sons, 1922, p. 547.

[7]Algermissen, Konrad. *Christian Denominations.* London: B. Herder Book Company, 1946, p. 812.

[8]Anson, Peter F. *Bishops at Large.* New York: October House, 1964, p. 32.

[9]*Ibid.*, p. 35-36.

[10]Ferrette, Jules. *The Eastern Liturgy of the Holy Catholic, Apostolic, Orthodox Church.* London: Simpkin, Marshall, & Co., 1866.

[11]Anson, p. 42-43.

[12]Jules Ferette, following ancient custom, took a religious name at his consecration, *i.e.*, Mar Julius.

[13]Anson, p. 145.

[14]*Ibid.*, p. 171-172.

[15]*Ibid.*, p. 178.

[16]Maynard, Theodore. *The Story of American Catholicism*. New York: Macmillan, 1941.

[17]*Ibid.*, p. 190.

[18]*Ibid.*, p. 228-229.

[19]Anson, p. 91.

[20]*Ibid.*, p. 97.

[21]*Ibid.*, p. 126-128.

[22]*Ibid.*, p. 430.

[23]Janowski, Robert W. *The Growth of a Church*. Scranton, PA: Straz Printery, 1965, p. 27.

[24]*Ibid.*, p. 27.

[25]Fox, Paul. *The Polish National Catholic Church*. Scranton, PA: School of Christian Living, n.d., p. 25.

[26]*Ibid.*, p. 28.

[27]Janowski, p. 39.

[28]Fox, p. 63.

[29]Klimczak, Joseph. *Bishop Francis Hodur and His Teachings*. Lowell, MA: St. Casimir's P.N.C. Church, 1969, p. 4-5.

BIBLIOGRAPHY
†

BOOKS

Algermission, Konrad. *Christian Denominations.* London: B. Herder Book Co., 1946.

Andrews, Theodore. *The Polish National Catholic Church.* London: S.P.C.K., 1953.

Anson, Peter. *Bishops at Large.* New York: October House, Inc., 1964.

Ellis, John Tracy. *American Catholicism.* Chicago: University of Chicago Press, 1956.

Fairweather, Eugene R. *The Oxford Movement.* New York: Oxford University Press, 1965.

Ferrette, Jules. *The Eastern Liturgy of the Holy Catholic Apostolic and Orthodox Church.* London: Simpkin, Marshall, & Co., 1866.

Fox, Paul. *The Polish National Catholic Church.* Scranton, PA: School of Christian Living, n.d.

Girondola, Anthony. *The Most Defiant Priest.* New York: Crown Publishers, 1968.

Grandi & Grandi. *The Story of the Church,* translated and edited by John Chapin. Garden City, NY: Hanover House, 1960.

Holman, John. *The Old Catholic Church of America.* Milwaukee, WI: The Old Catholic Church of America, 1977.

Hubensteiner, Benno. *Bayerische Geschichte.* München: Richard Pflaum Verlag, 1963.

Janowski, Robert. *The Growth of a Church.* Scranton, PA: Straz Printery, 1965.

Klimczak, Joseph. *Bishop Francis Hodur and His Teachings.* Lowell, MA: Privately Printed, 1969.

Magner, James A. *The Catholic Priest in the Modern World.* Milwaukee, WI: Bruce Publishing Co., 1957.

Maynard, Theodore. *The Story of American Catholicism.* New York: Macmillan Co., 1941.

Mills, Dorothy. *Renaissance and Reformation Times.* New York: G. P. Putnam's Sons, 1939.

Moss, C. B. *The Old Catholic Movement, Second Edition.* New York: Morehouse-Barlow Co., 1964.

Mourret, Fernand. *A History of the Catholic Church, Vol. 5,* translated by Newton Thompson. St. Louis, MO: B. Herder Book Co., 1955.

Overbeck, J. J. *Catholic Orthodox and Anglo-Catholicism.* London: AMS Press, New York, 1969 (reprinted from the 1866 edition).

Peck, W. G. *From Chaos to Catholicism.* New York: Macmillan Co., 1920.

Prüter, Hugo R. *The Theology of Congregationalism.* Flagler, CO: The Brownist Press, 1963.

Prüter, Hugo R. *Neo-Congregationalism, Third Edition.* Zuni, NM: St. Willibrord Press, 1973.

Prüter, Karl. *The Teachings of the Great Mystics.* Goffstown, NH: St. Willibrord's Press, 1969.

Prüter, Karl. *The Old Catholic Sourcebook.* New York: Garland Press & J. Gordon Melton Publishing, 1983.

Schultz, Paul. *A History of the Apostolic Succession of Archbishop Emile F. Rodriguez-Fairfield from the Mexican National Catholic Church, Iglesia Ortodoxa Católica Apostolica Mexicana.* Glendale, CA: Paul Schultz, 1983.

Terry-Thompson, A. C. *The History of the African Orthodox Church.* New York: The African Orthodox Church, 1956.

Tracy, Robert E. *American Bishop at the Vatican Council.* New York: McGraw-Hill Book Co., 1966.

Walker, Williston. *A History of the Christian Church.* New York: Charles Scribner's Sons, 1922.

Ward, Gary, L., ed. *Independent Bishops: An International Directory.* Detroit: Omnigraphics, 1990.

Whalen, William. *Separated Brethren.* Milwaukee, WI: Bruce Publishing Company, 1957.

NEWSPAPERS

Daily News, New York, December 9, 1960.
Daily Mirror, New York, December 9, 1960.

PAMPHLETS AND BOOKLETS

Dunn, Paul. *Christ Catholic Church: What Is It?* Highlandville, MO: St. Willibrord Press, n.d.

Hickman, Peter. *A Way of Being Catholic in Today's World.* The American Catholic Church, n.d.

Oehley, Raymond E. *What Is the Independent Catholic Church?* Harford: Independent Catholic Church, 1971.

Prüter, Karl. *Are You a Catholic Without Knowing It?* Zuni, NM: St. Willibrord's Press, 1971.

Prüter, Karl. *The House Church Movement.* Zuni, NM: St. Willibrord's Press, 1972.

Prüter, Karl. *The Story of Christ Catholic Church.* St. Willibrord's Press, 1981.

Prüter, Karl. *The Story of Christ Catholic Church, Second Edition.* Highlandville, MO: St. Willibrord Press, 1993.

Whalen, William. *The Polish National Catholic Church.* Chicago: Claretian Press, 1972.

THESIS

Ford, James Ishmael. *Episcopi Vagantes and the Challenge to Catholic Ministry.* A thesis presented to the Faculty of the Pacific School of Religion in partial fulfillment of the requirements for the degree of Master of Arts Berkeley Seminary, Berkeley, California, 1992.

INDEX
†

Africa, 84
African Orthodox Church, 5-6, 10-11, 65, 81-86
African Orthodox Church of the West, 84-85
Alaska, 61
Albanian Orthodox Church, 94
Aleutian Islands, 61
Alexandria, Patriarchate of, 17
Algermissen, Konrad, 111
Allmen, Bishop Robert, American Catholic Church, 6
Alvarez, Jules—SEE: Ferrette, Jules
American Catholic Church, 6, 9, 69, 82, 93, 108
American Catholicism (Maynard), 56
American Civil War, 57
American Old Catholic Church, 11
American Orthodox Church—SEE: Old Catholic Church
Amsterdam, Netherlands, 26
Ancient Catholic Church, 47
Anglican Church, 31-36, 37-39, 43-44, 48, 60-61, 63, 69, 88,
    109
Anglican Orders, 68
Anglo-Catholic Party, 34, 41
Anglo-Saxon Americans, 68
Anson, Peter F., 63, 65, 96, 111, 113
Antigua, West Indies, 81-82
Antioch, Patriarchate of, 17, 38, 46, 62-63, 88
Apostolicae Curae (Papal Bull), 35
apostolic succession, 35, 91
"Are You a Catholic Without Knowing It?" (Prüter), 96
Arian heresy, 17

Arizona, 96
Arkansas, 27, 81
Association for the Promotion of the Unity of Christendom, 37
Augustine, Bishop of Hippo, Saint, 17
Augustinian Order, 56
Augustus Caesar
Australia, 100
Austria, 20, 27
Autocephalous Church of the Apostolic Succession, 109
Autocephalous Movement, 5, 96
Autocephalous Orthodox Churches, 37-42
Awakening, 31
Babylon, See of, 26-27
Baier, Father Del, 102
Baltimore, Maryland, 52, 54-57, 75
Barbeau, Andrew, Bishop of Charismatic Catholic Church, 98
Barrow, Richard Grant, Father, 84
Bavaria, Germany, 20, 28, 90
Bekken, Dean, Archbishop of Liberal Catholic Church International, 103
Belchertown, Massachusetts, 88
Belfast, Northern Ireland, 46
Belgian Church, 60, 64
Belgium, 60
Benedict XIII, Pope of Rome, 27
Berwyn, Illinois, 88
Bethlehem, Israel, 14
Bishop Francis Hodur and His Teachings (Klimczak), 112, 114
Bishop W. H. Daw Seminary, 105-106
Bishops at Large (Anson), 111, 113
Bishops Extraordinary, 7
Blacks, 81-85
Blessed Trinity Church, Canada, 102-103
Board of Missions, Protestant Episcopal Church, 82
Bohatyretz, Nicholas, Metropolitan of Ukrainian Orthodox Church, 94
Book of Common Prayer (Anglican), 88

Book of Worship for Free Churches (Congregational), 88
Borgo Press, 5
Boston, Massachusetts, 90, 95-96
Bostwick, James Edward, 108
Bourbonnais, Illinois, 60
Brandreth, Henry, 97
Brantford, Ontario, Canada, 102
British Columbia, Canada, 103, 105
Broadstairs, England, 46
Brothers, Francis, Bishop-Abbot, 68
Brown, John, Bishop of Liberal Catholic Church of Ontario,
    103
Brown, Walter X., Bishop of Old Roman Catholic Church,
    108
Browne, Robert, Canon, 34, 55-57
Buffalo, New York, 64, 77
Butler, James Bernardt, Primate Metropolitan of African
    Orthodox Church, 85
Byeloruss, 94
Caesar Augustus, 14
California, 85, 109
Calkins, Raymond, Dr., 88
Cambridge, Massachusetts, 81
Canada, 60, 65, 68, 70, 97-106
Carfora, Carmel Henry, Archbishop of North American Old
    Roman Catholic Church, 10, 67-72
Carmelite Order, 60
Carroll, John, Roman Catholic Archbishop of Baltimore, 52,
    54-55
Cathedral Bookstore, Highlandville, Missouri, 100
Cathedral of the Prince of Peace, Highlandville, Missouri,
    97, 100
Catholic Apostolic Church, 47
The Catholic Priest (Prüter), 7
Celtic Catholic Church of the Utrecht Succession, 47, 103
Ceylon, 10, 62-63
Champaign, Illinois, 89
Charismatic Catholic Church, 98
Charleston, South Carolina, 56

119

Chicago, Illinois, 77, 82, 84-85, 88, 96-97
Chiniquy, Charles, Father, 60
Chippawa, Ontario, Canada, 102
Chiswick, England, 46
Christ—SEE: Jesus Christ
Christ Catholic Church, Diocese of Boston, 11, 90, 96
Christ Catholic Church, International, 11, 101-106
Christ Catholic Church (of the Americas and Europe), 6, 11, 89-90, 93-100, 109
Christ Catholic Mass, 99
Christian Catholic Church of Switzerland, 44
Christian Denominations (Algermissen), 111
Christocentric, 87
Chrysostom, John, St., 99
Church of England—SEE: Anglican Church
Church of Our Lady of Good Death, Chicago, Illinois, 82
Church of the Blessed Sacrament, Green Bay, Wisconsin, 61
Church of the Good Shepherd, New York, 82
Church of the Holy Mother of the Rosary, Buffalo, New York, 64
Church of the Holy Trinity, Nanticoke, Pennsylvania, 75
Church of the Precious Blood, Little Sturgeon, Wisconsin, 61
Church of the Transfiguration, Boston, Massachusetts, 95
Churches of the Apostolic Succession, 5
Cistercian Order, 65
Clerics of St. Viator, Bourbonnais, Illinois, 60
Cleveland, Ohio, 77
College of Saint-Laurent, Montréal, Canada, 60
Cologne, France, 62
Colorado, 95
Columbus, New Mexico, 97
Commission for Work Among the Colored People, 82, 84
Community of Christian Brothers, Namur, Belgium, 60
The Confirmation Workbook and Catechism, 7
Congregational Chapel, Islington, England, 45-46
Congregational Christian Church, 87-89
Congregational Church, Kings Weigh House, England, 40
Congregational Church, Sheffield, Massachusetts, 88
Congregationalism, 87-91

Congress of Munich, 43
Conservative Congregational Conference, 89
Constantine I, Emperor of Rome, 17
Constantinople, 17
Council of Constance, 20
Council of Nicaea, 17
Council of Trent, 9, 20, 27
Croyden, England, 46
Czechoslovakian immigrants to America, 93
Dale (Congregational historian), 91
Daw, W. Harry, Bishop of Liberal Catholic Church of
    Ontario, 101, 103, 105
de Landas Berghes et de Rache, Bishop of the Old Roman
    Catholic Church of England, Prince, 10, 68
de Lisle, Ambrose Phillips, 40
"Declaration of Autonomy and Independence" (Mathew),
    46, 99
Deering, New Hampshire, 96
Demers, Joseph, Bishop of Liberal Catholic Church
    International, 103-104
Deming, New Mexico, 97
Denver, Colorado, 95
Deventer, See of, 10, 27-28, 61
Dickson City, Pennsylvania, 76
The Directory of Bishops of the Autocephalous Churches of
    the Apostolic Succession (Prüter), 6
Diocese of Boston, 95-97
Diocese of New Mexico and the East, 95
Diocese of Vermont, 110
A Divine Liturgy for Free Churches (Prüter), 88
The Divine Liturgy: The Mass for Orthodox Use, 7
Doctrine of Papal Infallibility—SEE: Papal Infallibility
Döllinger, Ignaz von, Chaplain to Ludwig II of Bavaria, 28
Dominican Mission, 38
Dover, New Jersey, 94
Druidic Order, 39
Dublin, Ireland, 56
Duncan, Margaret (later Mathew), 44
Dunellen, New Jersey, 94

Dunleavy, Frederick, Archbishop of Ontario, Old Roman Catholic Church of Canada, 97-98, 104-105
Dutch Churches, 21-22, 25-27, 45, 64
Duval, Wisconsin, 64
Dyckesville, Wisconsin, 61, 63
The Early Church, 13-18
Easter, 15
Eastern Christians, 37
Eastern Church Association, 37
Eastern Churches, 37
The Eastern Liturgy of the Holy Catholic, Apostolic, Orthodox Church Adapted for Use in the West (Ferrette), 9
Eastern Orthodox Churches, 83
Ecumenical Movement, 88
Ely, Bishop of, 43
Emesa, See of, 38
Endich Theological Seminary, Long Island, New York, 83
England, John, Roman Catholic Bishop of Charleston, 56-57
England, 31-36, 38-41, 43-49
English Catholic Church, 46-47
Episcopal Church, 60-62, 64, 68, 70, 81-82, 95, 108-109
Erastian nature, 34
Essenes, 13
Etobicoke, Canada, 103
The Euchologion of The Eastern Liturgy Adapted for Use in the West (Ferrette), 38-39
Evangelical and Reformed Church, 89
Evangelical Catholic Church, 40-41
Evangelical Movement and Revival, 31-33, 35
Facione, Bishop Francis P., 108
Fagan, Roman Catholic Bishop of Meath, 26
Federation of Independent Catholic Churches, 100
Fellowship of Independent Catholic and Orthodox Bishops, 106
Ferrette, Jules (Jules Alvarez or Mar Julius I), Bishop of Iona and Metropolitan of the Independent Catholic Church of Ceylon, Goa, and India, 9-10, 37-40, 62-63
Fitzgerald, Bishop of Little Rock, 27
Fox, Paul, 112-113

122

France, 21, 25-26, 59-60, 62, 65
Franciscan Order, 56
Franco-Prussian War, 27
Free Catholic Church, 40, 47, 87-92
Free Catholic Movement, 87-92, 96
Free Greek Orthodox Church, 106
French missionaries in America, 51-52, 54-57, 73-74
From Faith to Faith (Orchard), 41
Froude, Richard Hurrell, 32-34
Gallagher, Simon Felix, Father and Doctor, 55-57
Gallican Catholic Church, France, 60
Garden of Saints, Highlandville, Missouri, 100
Garvey, Marcus, 82
Gauthier, Father, 61, 64
German immigrants to America, 53-55, 93
Germany, 10, 27-28, 43-44, 71, 90
Glasgow, Scotland, 44
Glorietta, New Mexico, 96
Goa, 10, 62
Gossett, W. Wolfgang, Father, 98
Grafton, Anglican Bishop, 61, 63
Greeks, 14
Green, Episcopal Bishop of New York, 82
Green Bay, Wisconsin, 61-62, 64
Gregory IV, Greek Orthodox Patriarch of Antioch, 46
The Growth of a Church (Janowski), 112, 114
The Guardian (newspaper), 46
Guinness Book of World Records, 97
Gul, Gerardus, Archbishop of Utrecht, 10, 45, 88
Haarlem, See of, 27
Hamilton, Ontario, Canada, 101, 104
Hampton, Charles, Bishop of Liberal Catholic Church
    International, 101
Hatherly, Stephen Georgeson, 40
Haves, Father (Franciscan), 56
Herford, Ulric Vernon, Bishop, 40-41
Herzog, Edward, Christian Catholic Bishop of Switzerland,
    44-45, 60

Heykamp, Hermann, Old Catholic Bishop of Deventer, 10, 28, 61
Hickman, Peter, Bishop of American Catholic Church, 108
Highlandville, Missouri, 97, 100
Hinkson, G. Duncan, Archbishop and Primate Co-Adjutor of African Orthodox Church, 6, 84-85, 97
Hippo, 17
A History of the Christian Church (Walker), 111, 115
A History of the Old Catholic Church (Prüter), 5, 7, 96
A History of War and Peace (Prüter), 100
Hobbs, New Mexico, 95
Hodur, Francis, Bishop of Polish National Catholic Church, 10, 75-80
Holland, 21-23, 25-26—SEE ALSO: Netherlands
Holy Catholic, Apostolic, Orthodox Church, 38
Holy Eastern Orthodox Catholic and Apostolic Church in North America, 106
Holy Family Boys Home, Niagara Falls, Canada, 102
Holy Supper, 16
Holy Trinity Church, London, England, 44
Holy Trinity Church, Nanticoke, Pennsylvania, 75
Homs, Bishop of Emesa, 38
Horton, Douglas, Dr., 88
"The House Church Movement" (Prüter), 96
Houston, Texas, 84
Huntington Beach, California
Hus, John, 20
Iglesia Ortodoxa Católica Mexicana, 70
Ignatius Jacob II, Syrian Jacobite Patriarch of Antioch, 38, 62
Illinois, 60, 77, 82, 84-85, 88-90, 96-97
Independent Bishops: An International Directory, 6
Independent Catholic Church of America, 52, 56-57
Independent Catholic Church of Ceylon, Goa, and India, 62
Independent Episcopal Church, 81-82
India, 10, 62-63
Indulgences, 20
Iona, See of, 9, 38-39, 62
Ireland, 26, 56
Irish missionaries in America, 51-52, 54-57, 73-74

Irish parishioners in America, 55, 73-74
Islington, England, 45-46
Italian immigrants to America, 67-68
Italian missionaries, 67
Italian National Episcopal Church, 67
Italy, 21, 27, 67
Itasca, Illinois, 90
Janowski, Robert W., 112, 114
Jansen, Cornelius, 25
Jansenists, 21, 25
Jaroshevich, Konstantin, Archbishop, 94
Jefferson Medical College, 81
Jenkins, John, Bishop of Liberal Catholic Church
    International, 103
Jerusalem, 17
Jesuits, 21, 25
Jesus Christ, 9, 13, 15-17, 21, 79, 87, 91
Jews, 14
John Paul II, Pope of Rome, 110
John the Baptist, Saint, 13, 15
Jones, Christopher William, Bishop and Abbot of Christ
    Catholic Church, 96
Joseph, Father—SEE: Vilatte, Joseph
Joseph, Saint, 14
Judaism, 14
Judea, 13
Julius I Ferrette, Mar—SEE: Ferrette, Jules
Kaminski, Stephen, Bishop of the Old Catholic Church, 64-
    65, 77
Keating, Arthur, Father, 103
Keble, John, 33-34
Kelly, Joseph, Father, 70
Kelly, Patrick, Roman Catholic Bishop of Richmond,
    Virginia, 56
King, Franzo, Bishop of African Orthodox Church, 85
King's Weigh House, London, 40
Klawiter, Rev. Father, 76
Klimovicz, Joseph, Patriarch of Orthodox Catholic
    Patriarchate of America, 94

Klimczak, Joseph, 112, 114
Kozlowski, Antoni, Bishop of the Old Catholic Church, 64, 77
Krupski, Bronislaw, Father, 78
Krys, Jacob, Father, 26
Kurdistan, 38
Lambert, W. Noel, Father, 45
Laplante, J. Gerard, Bishop of Old Catholic Church of British Columbia, 105
LaPointe, Jean, Bishop, 97
Las Cruces, New Mexico, 97
Latin Mass, 110
Latin Rite, 62
Le Roy, Illinois, 97
Ledochowski, Roman Catholic Cardinal, 75
Leo XIII, Pope of Rome, 35
Liberal Catholic Church International, 98-99, 103-104
Liberal Catholic Church of England, 47
Liberal Catholic Church of Ontario, 11, 98-99, 101-102
Lincoln, Bishop of, 43
Lincoln, Nebraska, 106
Listen Pilgrim (Jones), 96
Lithuanian immigrants to America, 68, 93
Little Rock, See of, 27
Little Sturgeon, Wisconsin, 61
Liturgical Movement, 88
Lloyd, Archbishop of the American Catholic Church, 69
London, England, 40, 44
Long Island, New York, 83
Look Around, Pilgrim (Jones), 96
Lopez, Father, 64
Loyson, Hyacinthe, Father, 60
Ludwig II, King of Bavaria, 28
Luther, Martin, 20
Lutheran Church, 102, 136
Macedonian Call, 97
Magdalen College, 37
Maine, 96
Manitoba, Canada, 104

Marchenna, Richard A., Supreme Primate of North American Old Roman Catholic Church, 70

Marechal, Ambrose, Roman Catholic Archbishop of Baltimore, 55-57

Mary, Saint, 14

Maryland, 52, 54-57, 75

Massachusetts, 81, 88, 90, 94-96

Mather, Howard, Congregational Bishop, 88

Mathew, Arnold Harris, Bishop of Old Catholic Church of England, later English Catholic Church, later Old Roman Catholic Church (of America), 10, 43-48, 65, 68, 88, 94, 99

Matthews, Edward Murray, Bishop of Liberal Catholic Church, 101

May, F. S., Rev., 43

Maynard, Theodore, 52, 56

McCourt, Thomas, Bishop of Liberal Catholic Church of Ontario, 103

McGuire, George Alexander, Bishop of the African Orthodox Church, 10, 65, 81-85

Meath, Ireland, 26

Melchizek, M. S., Bishop of Free Greek Orthodox Church, 106

Mercian Orthodox Catholic Church, 105

Meredith, Robert, Father, 98

Mesopotamia, 38

Messiah, 13, 15

Methodist Church and Methodism, 31-36, 109

México City, D.F., México, 70

México, D.F., 89

Middle Ages, 19-23

Middle East, 14

Midwest Congregational Christian Fellowship, 89

Miller, William Russell, Archbishop of African Orthodox Church, 84

Miraglia-Culiotti, Paolo, Bishop of the Italian National Episcopal Church, 67

Mississauga, Oakville, Canada, 103-104

Missouri, 97-98, 100

Mithra, 14
monasteries, 19
Monastery of Our Lady of Reconciliation, Glorietta, New Mexico, 96
Montréal, Québec, Canada, 60
Morgan, Richard Williams, Bishop, 39
Moss, C. B., 96, 111, 114
Mouthy, Father, 64
Mullan, William Donald, Archbishop of Liberal Catholic Church of Ontario and Christ Catholic Church International, 11, 98, 102-103, 105-106
Munich, Germany, 10, 28, 43
mystery cults, 14
Namur, Belgium, 60
Nanticoke, Pennsylvania, 75
Napoleonic times, 60
National Association of Congregational Christian Churches, 89
National Catholic Diocese in North America, 67-68
National Old Catholic Church, 6
Neale, Dr., Roman Catholic Archbishop, 37, 55
Near East, 38
Nebraska, 106
Netherlands, 21-23, 25-26
New Brunswick, New Jersey, 94
New Hampshire, 88, 96
New Jersey, 94-95
New Mexico, 95-97
New Perspectives, 108
New York, 64, 77, 82-83, 108
Newman, John Henry, Cardinal, 33-35
Newport, Oregon, 98
Niagara Falls (Diocese of), Canada, 70, 98-99, 102-103, 106
Noli, Fan Stylin, Archbishop of Albanian Orthodox Church, 94
North American Old Roman Catholic Church, 70, 109
North Berwyn Congregational Church, 89
Novus Ordo, 99
Nurse, Gladston St. Clair, Archbishop of African Orthodox Church, 84-85

Nybledh, Carl A., Bishop of the American Orthodox Church, 10, 82
Oakville, Ontario, Canada, 103
Oconomowoc, Wisconsin, 108
O'Halleran, Richard, Father, 45
Ohio, 67, 77
Old Catholic Church Chronology, 9-12
Old Catholic Church of America, 6, 10-11, 29, 59-65, 69, 77, 90, 94, 107-110
Old Catholic Church in Europe, 6, 25-30, 62, 77
Old Catholic Church of Austria, 28
Old Catholic Church of British Columbia, 105
Old Roman Catholic Church, 108
Old Roman Catholic Church of Canada, 97
Old Catholic Church of Czechoslovakia, 28
Old Catholic Church of England, 10, 29, 34, 43-50
Old Catholic Church of France, 28
Old Catholic Church of Germany, 10, 28, 45
Old Catholic Church of Holland, 22-23, 25-27, 44-45—SEE ALSO: Dutch Church
Old Catholic Church of Poland, 28
Old Catholic Church of Switzerland, 44-45, 60-61
Old Catholic Church of Yugoslavia, 28
Old Catholic Congress (Cologne, 1890), 62
Old Catholic Councils, 10, 28
The Old Catholic Missal and Liturgy (Mathew and Gul), 88
The Old Catholic Movement: Its Origins and History (Moss), 111, 114
The Old Catholic Sourcebook, 6-7
Old Catholicism, 6-7, 15, 20, 34, 43
Old Roman Catholic Church in North America, 10, 67-71, 108
Old Roman Catholic Church of America, 67-71
Old Roman Catholic Church of England, 47, 67
Old Roman Catholic Church of Germany, 71
Old Roman Catholic Church of the United States and Canada, 70
Oliver, Philip Aliva, Bishop of Christ Catholic Church, 97
Ontario, Canada, 97, 101-104

Orchard, William, Dr., Pastor of Kings Weigh House, 40
Order of Antioch, 88
Oregon, 98
Orford, New Hampshire, 88
Orthodox Catholic Patriarchate of America, 94
Orthodox Church, 17, 37-41, 46, 109
Orthodox Western Catholic Church, 39-40
Ottawa, Ontario, Canada, 104
Overbeck, J. Joseph, Father, 39-40
Oxford, England, 46
Oxford Movement, 9, 31-36, 48
Palmer, William, Deacon, 37
Papacy, 20-22, 25—SEE ALSO: Popes
Papal Infallibility, 27, 44, 110
Papal States, 19
Paris, France, 26, 59
Pentecostal Church, 99
Pérez y Budar, José Joachín, Archbishop of Mexico City of
    Iglesia Ortodoxa Católica Mexicana, 70
Pennsylvania, 74-76, 88-89, 94, 109
Persia, 26
Petite Église, France, 59-60
Pharisees, 13
Philadelphia, Pennsylvania, 89, 94
Pilgrim Fathers, 87
Pilgrim Missionary Society, 90
Pittsburgh, Pennsylvania, 88
Pius IX, Pope of Rome, 27
Poland, 78
Polish Catholic Church, 65
Polish immigrants to America, 68, 73-80, 93
Polish language, 78-79
Polish missionaries to America, 73-80
Polish National Catholic Church (PNCC), 5, 10, 65, 73-80,
    93
The Polish National Catholic Church (Fox), 112-113
Polish Old Catholic Church, 11, 64-65, 94
Polish Roman Catholic Church, 74-75
Pon-Colbert (Abbey of), Versailles, France, 65
Pontiff—SEE: Pope

Pope (Head of Roman Catholic Church), 19, 22, 43, 65
Port Royal, France, 25
Presbyterians, 38, 60
The Priest's Handbook (Prüter), 7
Protestant Episcopal Church, 82
Protestant Reformation—SEE: Reformation
Protestant Churches, 21, 51-52, 79, 99
Prüter, Karl (Hugo R.), Bishop of Old Catholic Church, 5-7, 88-90, 96-100, 105, *passim*
Pusey, Edward Bouverie, Dr., 38
Raible, Paul, Bishop of American Orthodox Church—Old Catholic, 11
Reformation, 19-24
Reinkens, Josef Hubert, Bishop of German Old Catholic Church, 10, 28
Republic, Missouri, 89
Resch, Francis X., Bishop of Old Catholic Church of America, 11
restricto mentalis, 28
Resurrection, 15
Reuter, Caesarius, Father, 54-55
Rhode Island, 96
Richmond, Virginia, 56
Ritual Commission, 44-45
Robertson, W. E. J., Archbishop of African Orthodox Church, 83-84
Robinson, Bishop Gene, 110
Rogers, Hubert A., Primate of North American Old Roman Catholic Church, 70
Roman Catholic Church, 22-23, 26-27, 34-35, 38-40, 44-46, 51-57, 59-60, 64-65, 67-69, 74-75, 78-80, 93, 95, 102, 110
Roman Catholic Church in America, 51-58
Roman Diocese, Buffalo, New York, 77
Roman Empire, 13-14, 17
Roman Government, 16
Rome, 14, 17, 19, 21-23, 26-28, 34-35, 55-56, 60, 63-64, 67, 73-77
Rotterdam, 23

Russell, John Henry, Bishop of Liberal Catholic Church of Ontario, 102-103
Russia, Patriarchate of, 37, 39
Russian Orthodox Church, 61
Salt Lake City, Utah, 97-98
"same sex" marriages, 109
San Francisco, California, 85
Sawyer, Raymond, Bishop, 97-98
Scarborough, Ontario, Canada, 104
Scotland, 44
Scranton, Pennsylvania, 74-76
Second Synod (PNCC), 77-78
Sheffield, Massachusetts, 88
Shelley, Gerard George, Primate of Old Roman Catholic Church in North America, 70
The Simple Service Book, 7
Smith, Daniel, Bishop of Christ Catholic Church, 95
Society of Free Catholics, 40
South Carolina, 56
South Hero, Vermont, 104
South River, New Jersey, 94-95
Spanish missionaries, 51
Springfield, Massachusetts, 94
Springfield, Missouri, 7
Spruit, Meri Louise, Matriarch of Fellowship of Independent Catholic and Orthodox Bishops, 106
St. Adelbert's Church, Dickson City, Pennsylvania, 76
St. Augustine's Cathedral, Chicago, Illinois, 84-85, 97
St. Barnabas Christ Catholic Mission, Newport, Oregon, 98
St. Bartholomew's Episcopal Church, Cambridge, Massachusetts, 81
St. Bridget's Church, Toronto, Canada, 103
St. Catherines, Ontario, Canada, 104
St. Cuthbert's Church, Oakville, Ontario, Canada, 103
St. Francis Church, Chippewa, Canada, 102
St. Elias Orthodox Catholic Seminary, 106
St. Francis Liturgy, 99
St. Francis of Assisi Church, Hamilton, Ontario, Canada, 101
St. Joseph's Church, Walhain, Wisconsin, 64
St. Jude's Church, Etobicoke, Canada, 103

St. Louis Cathedral, Green Bay, Wisconsin, 63-64
St. Luke's Church, Niagara Falls, Ontario, Canada, 102
St. Luke Magazine, 105
St. Mary's Church, Baltimore, Maryland, 55
St. Mary's Church, Duval, Wisconsin, 64
St. Paul's Church, Denver, Colorado, 95
St. Paul's Church, Hobbs, New Mexico, 95
St. Paul's Church, Sweets, Antigua, 82
St. Peter's Church, Baltimore, Maryland, 54-55
St. Peter's Seminary at Partickhill, Glasgow, Scotland, 44
St. Raphael's Church, Vancouver, B.C., 105-106
St. Stanislaus Parish, Scranton, Pennsylvania, 76
The St. Willibrord Journal, 6
St. Willibrord Press, 7, 96-97
St. Willibrord's Cathedral, Islington, England, 45-46
Stamford, Ontario, Canada, 102
Starazewski, Felix, Father, 95
Starkey, Cyrus A., Bishop of North American Old Roman
    Catholic Church, 70
Steenoven, Cornelius, Archbishop of Utrecht, 9, 27
The Story of American Catholicism (Maynard), 112, 114
Sweeting, Stafford James, Archbishop of African Orthodox
    Church, 6, 84
Sweets, Antigua, 82
Switzerland, 27, 44, 60
Synod of Baltimore, 75
synagogues, 14
Syrian Jacobite Church, Antioch, 37, 62
Syrian Orthodox Church, 38
Tarentum, Pennsylvania, 88
The Teachings of the Great Mystics (Prüter), 96
The Temple (Orchard), 40
Terry-Thompson, A. C., Father, 84
Texas, 84
Theosophical Society, 47
Thiesen, Joseph Maria, Archbishop of Old Roman Catholic
    Church of Germany, 71
Thomas, Illtyd, Bishop of Celtic Catholic Church, 103
Tiberius Caesar, Emperor of Rome, 13

Toronto, Ontario, Canada, 103
Tractarian Movement, 35
Traditional Catholic Church, 109-110
Transfiguration, Feast of, 47
Traunwallchen, Upper Bavaria, 90
Tridentine Mass, 99
Trustee Controversy, 9, 52-53, 74-75
trusteeism in America, 52-53, 74
Ukrainian Orthodox Church, 94
Uniate Churches, 40
Unitarian Church, 31, 44, 87-88
United Church of Christ, 88-89
United Negro Improvement Association of the World, 82
Upper Bavaria, 90
Utah, 97-98
Utrecht, See of, 9-10, 21-23, 25-27, 45-46, 48, 56, 59, 61, 68
van Neercassel, Archbishop of Utrecht, 26
Vancouver, B.C., Canada, 106
Varlet, Dominique Marie, Bishop of Babylon, 9, 26
Vatican Council I (1869-1870), 9, 27-28, 43
Vatican Council II, 48
Vermont, 104
Versailles, France, 65
Vilatte, Joseph René, Archbishop of Old Catholic Church of
    America, 10, 59-67, 71, 73, 77, 82-83, 94
Virginia, 56
Vladimir, Russian Orthodox Bishop of Alaska and the
    Aleutian Islands, 61-62
von Döllinger, Ignaz—SEE: Döllinger, Ignaz von
Walhain, Wisconsin, 64
Walker, Williston, 111, 115
Wedgewood, Father, 47
Wesley, John, 33
West Indies, 81-82, 84
West Virginia, 67-68
Western Church, 19-20
Western Europe, 38
Whissell, Larry, Father, 103
Williamowicz, Peter M., Bishop of Old Catholic Church, 94

Willoughby, Frederick Samuel, Bishop of the English
    Catholic Church, later Liberal Catholic Church, 46-47
Windsor, Ontario, Canada, 104
Winnipeg, Manitoba, Canada, 104
Wisconsin, 60-64, 109
Wolodymyr II, Head of Holy Eastern Orthodox Catholic and
    Apostolic Church, 106
Yugoslavia, 28
Zhurawetzky, Peter A., Archbishop of Christ Catholic
    Church, 11, 90, 94-96
Zielonka, Joseph, Archbishop of Polish Old Catholic
    Church, 11, 94-95
Zoroastrians, 14

ABOUT THE AUTHOR
†

BISHOP KARL PRÜTER was born in 1920 in Poughkeepsie, New York. Following high school there he completed undergraduate work at Boston's Northeastern University, and then earned his master's degree in divinity at the Lutheran Theological Seminary in Philadelphia. After starting his ecclesiastical career as a congregational minister, he wrote two books, the second of which, *Neo-Congregationalism*, was later revised to include a chapter relating the personal sojourn that brought him to the Old Catholic Movement.

In 1967 Bishop Prüter was consecrated bishop of Christ Catholic Church, and the church, under his leadership, has significantly influenced the entire Old Catholic Movement. He served as presiding bishop of Christ Catholic Church from 1967 to June 1991, when he then became suffragan bishop in order to have more time to devote to spiritual writing and to promoting the retreat movement. Throughout his work in the church, Bishop Prüter has conducted literally hundreds of retreats for both Protestant and Catholic groups.

Along with having written scores of religious pamphlets, Bishop Prüter has also authored eight books, among them *The Teachings of the Great Mystics, A History of the Old Catholic Church, The Priest's Handbook*, and, most recently, *One Day with God* (Borgo Press, 1991), a self-instructional guide to spiritual retreats. He currently resides in Springfield, Missouri, where he serves the Cathedral of the Prince of Peace in Highlandville, which is listed in the *Guinness Book of World Records* as the planet's smallest cathedral, measuring 14 x 17 feet and seating fifteen people.